SOVEREIGNTY - THE RESTORATION OF SANITY

"If you wish to converse with me, first, define your terms."

Voltaire 1764

CW01500749

T he Title of this book, the word Sovereignty - has been and will be much discussed.

Sovereignty, here, specifically refers to the state or quality of being Sovereign in its adjectival meaning describing an entity that is independent and self-governing. As such when it relates to the individual it is a relative appraisal of a person's self-determinism.

Self-determinism is here defined as that spiritual quality of having the ability to exert one's own power of choice over whatever area of life one chooses.

Restoration as used here, is the act of returning the quality of something, physical or spiritual to its original, or native state.

Sanity has been described as the ability to differentiate between and recognise differences, similarities and identities.

It could be said to be the measure of how ably an individual helps things that assist survival and resists things that inhibit survival.

The ability to discern right from wrong is to be of sound mind - sane.

At the end of this book, you may find yourself asking:

"Am I a Sovereign Being?"

I hope the pages that follow help you to arrive at that conclusion in an interesting and sometimes entertaining way. I am sure you will make some conclusions about yourself and others.

We are now on a journey and an adventure together.

I hope you enjoy it.

We have cast off for an unknown destination.

Fair Winds,

Mike Fairclough

SOVEREIGNTY

- John Mappin -
The Restoration of Sanity

Mike Fairclough

Fisher King Publishing

SOVEREIGNTY - John Mappin - The Restoration of Sanity

Published by
Fisher King Publishing
www.fisherkingpublishing.co.uk

Copyright © Mike Fairclough 2025

Trade Paperback ISBN: 978-1-916776-88-3
Hardcover ISBN: 978-1-916776-89-0
Ebook ISBN: 978-1-916776-90-6

For Charlie

Contents

INTRODUCTION

A Hero at the Crossroad

There are men who pass quietly through history, and there are men who seem born to stand at its crossroads again and again. John Mappin is of the latter kind. His life has carried the pattern of the mythic hero, not as legend but as living reality; stepping forward whenever civilisation itself teeters on the brink. In an age that has lost its bearings, he has become a symbol of restoration, of the stubborn return of sanity in a world intoxicated by lies.

History has a way of disguising its turning points until much later, when hindsight makes everything obvious. But there are moments when you can feel the ground shift beneath your feet; moments when private choices become public battles, and when one man's stand captures something far larger than himself. John Mappin stands at such a moment now.

In Britain, the migrant crisis dominates the headlines. Yet Mappin's defiance against turning Camelot Castle into a migrant hotel is not new. His stand first drew widespread attention in 2022, when it was picked up across the mainstream press and became a story that everyone seemed to know. Since then, it has resurfaced again and again, most recently in September 2025, when the Daily Mail and the Express carried it once more. What began as a decision rooted in national sovereignty and integrity has long since become a touchstone; a symbol of resistance to imposed decline and the defence of Britain's right to remain itself. That symbolism did not stop at Britain's borders. Across the Atlantic during the 2015-16 presidential campaign, President Donald Trump's team and family recognised in Mappin, a kindred soul, a man willing to endure ridicule and attack in order to stand firm on questions of nationhood, control of borders and the restoration of a country. Their philosophical alignment grew from that shared conviction: that a country which cannot defend its own home, and embrace its basic founding principles, will soon cease to be a home at all.

The assassination of Charlie Kirk on September 10th, 2025, a close friend of both Mappin and President Trump, underscored the cost of speaking freely in an age of deception. For Mappin, Kirk's death was not only a personal blow but also a grim confirmation that the stakes are life and death. The struggle for sovereignty, truth and civilisation is no abstraction; it is personal, and it is perilous.

I first met John Mappin in February 2023, at the Carlton Club in London. It was intended as a private gathering, with no press and no cameras, yet word inevitably reached the outside world. Mappin had brought together more than one hundred and forty of the sharpest political and cultural minds at a moment when honest debate about Covid and the mRNA rollout was still smothered by fear. The purpose was not spectacle but substance; to support genuine scientific discussion, to weigh the evidence, and to examine the grave consequences of stifling free speech at the very moment it was most needed.

In that room were physicians and scientists who had risked everything to warn the public: Dr. Robert Malone, Dr. Ryan Cole, Dr. Aseem Malhotra. There were firebrand voices of Europe such as Eva Vlaardingerbroek and political figures like Andrew Bridgen, who had faced ostracism in Westminster. Diplomats and press attachés had come too, emissaries from international embassies and even presidential families. And then there was Nigel Farage, who may yet lead Britain, lending his presence that evening in defiance of the silence imposed elsewhere.

The event showed me something I had not realised until that night. Mappin was not just a unique businessman with a gift for headlines. He was a connector, a catalyst, someone willing to use his network, which reached from Camelot Castle to Mar-a-Lago, to bring truth-tellers together at a time when others kept their heads down.

Today, the word most often attached to him is 'hero.' It appears beneath articles in the mainstream press, in the comment threads of ordinary citizens, in the speeches of allies from Washington to Westminster. Mappin himself has resisted the title. He is confident without myth, a man who does not seek to be elevated. Yet the pattern of the heroic archetype clings to him all the same, because his story rhymes with something ancient. Arthur. Achilles. Odysseus. These figures survive not because they were flawless, but because they remind us that civilisation depends on courage, not comfort.

In my own books and talks I have returned often to this question of the heroic archetype, to the endurance of grit and resilience in the face of trial. My writing has drawn on Homer's *Odyssey*, on Joseph Campbell's exploration of the hero's quest, and on the mythologies of cultures across the world. As Campbell observed, the hero is rarely one who seeks the role, but one compelled by circumstance to accept it. In that sense, what I see in John Mappin is not self-proclamation but the recurrence of an ancient pattern. The man who acts because it is right, not because it is noticed.

This book is not a neutral biography. I write as an advocate, as one who has also paid the price of dissent. I have been cancelled, smeared, and silenced for speaking truths others wished buried. That is why I recognise the cost of Mappin's stand, and why his alliance with President Donald Trump, his friendship with Charlie Kirk, and his fight for Britain's soul matter far beyond the headlines.

His friendships stretch in unexpected directions. To Candace Owens, America's uncompromising voice of resistance; to Hollywood figures such as John Travolta, who have carried influence far beyond the screen; and to artists and musicians whose work still dares to speak of beauty, truth, and civilisation. These worlds rarely meet, yet in Mappin's orbit they converge. Politics, celebrity, and art. Spheres that normally repel one another, are here drawn into a single constellation of purpose.

Charlie Kirk often said the only way to find truth was to hear all sides without fear. That spirit runs through these pages. This is not hagiography. It is testimony to the power of sovereignty, sanity, and the heroic virtues embodied in a man who refuses to bend. What I discovered in tracing Mappin's journey astonished me. That meeting at the Carlton Club was only the beginning.

The Fortress of Ideas

John Mappin does not see the world as most men do. Where politicians speak of policies and pundits chatter about economics, he looks deeper, to the philosophies that either enslave or set nations free. At the heart of his crusade is a conviction that psychiatry, far from being a science of healing, has become a corrosive creed that strips man of soul and sovereignty, fuelling wars, tyranny and division. Against this stands his unyielding belief in the dignity of the individual and the sacred right of nations to remain sovereign. From Camelot Castle he has built more than a fortress of stone; he has forged a crossroads where leaders, thinkers, and visionaries gather.

I have known John for several years and have seen firsthand what he has achieved. I have witnessed the extraordinary network he has built at Camelot, drawing figures from across the world into conversations that ripple far beyond Cornwall's cliffs. There are moments when those conversations have likely stayed the hand of conflict, even averted wars, altering the direction of history itself.

To step into Mappin's world is to encounter not only a fortress of ideas, but a watchman at Camelot's gates; a man who sees the hidden engines of power, who dares to confront them, and who stands sentinel in an age teetering between freedom and control.

Philosophy: The Engine of History

At the heart of John Mappin's thinking is a conviction that philosophy, more than economics, politics, or raw power, is the true engine of history. He argues that behind every triumph or disaster in human affairs lies a set of ideas, and that the quality of those ideas, grounded either in truth and liberty or in coercion and falsehood, determines whether societies flourish in peace or collapse into conflict.

For Mappin, this is not an abstract reflection but a framework for understanding the crises of the modern world. He views today's wars, cultural upheavals, and ideological divisions as products of competing philosophies, each with radically different visions of truth, freedom, and human dignity. From his perspective, what plays out on battlefields or in parliaments is ultimately secondary to the deeper struggle over ideas.

Mappin often points to history to illustrate this conviction. He sees the Magna Carta, the Enlightenment, and the founding principles of modern democracies as examples of how philosophies rooted in individual dignity and reason lifted humanity out of oppression and poverty. Conversely, he regards the totalitarianisms of the twentieth century, whether fascism or communism, as catastrophic examples of what happens when flawed philosophies deny the individual's capacity for reason and replace it with force, dogma, or nihilism.

He also stresses that philosophy is not confined to great leaders or intellectuals. In his view, every person contributes to the philosophical fabric of society, whether through parenting, education, civic participation, or public debate. Ideas, he argues, filter down into everyday decisions, shaping the course of nations.

Central to his outlook is a warning - bad philosophy is seductive. It thrives on groupthink, fear and resentment, and it spreads most easily in times when dissent is silenced, or critical thought suppressed. For Mappin, the digital age has intensified this danger, turning social media echo chambers into accelerants of division and conflict.

Yet he insists that philosophy is not only the root of conflict but also the path to peace. He draws inspiration from figures such as Gandhi, Wilberforce, Rochefoucauld, Rousseau and Václav Havel, who proved that societies can be transformed through the force of ideas rather than violence. For Mappin, peace is not utopian. It is practical, provided humanity chooses philosophies that honour truth, liberty, and respect for the individual. This, he believes, is the crossroads of our age. In his view, the future of all civilisation depends less on technology or wealth than on whether we adopt a philosophy of freedom and truth, or one of division and control. As he often puts it, wars begin in the minds of men, and so too must the defences of peace.

Psychiatry as a Destructive Ideology

A defining element of Mappin's philosophy is his conviction that psychiatry is not simply a flawed branch of medicine but a destructive ideology with global consequences.

In his writings, he describes psychiatry as a hidden force behind many of the wars, tyrannies, and cultural breakdowns of the modern era. Where most commentators look to economics, politics, or military strategy to explain conflict, Mappin points to a deeper driver: a philosophy that reduces human beings to chemical processes, strips away the notion of soul or spirit, and legitimises control, manipulation, and even extermination.

For Mappin, history provides the evidence. He sees the Holocaust not merely as a political crime but as an atrocity with psychiatric roots, tracing back to the eugenics theories of Sir Francis Galton and the psychiatrists of Nazi Germany who first deemed certain lives 'unworthy of life.' In his telling, the concentration camps were foreshadowed by psychiatric wards where so-called 'defectives' were killed under the guise of science. After the war, he argues, psychiatry did not disappear but expanded, feeding into programmes such as the CIA's MKUltra and later becoming a tool of repression on both sides of the Iron Curtain.

Mappin extends this analysis into the present. He sees psychiatry's influence in the way governments manage dissent, through diagnoses, forced medication, or social labelling, and in how wars are framed, with enemies dehumanised and entire populations pathologised to justify violence. Whether in Ukraine, the Middle East, or Western democracies, he contends that psychiatric theories of behaviour and control have been weaponised to maintain instability, escalate division, and keep populations compliant. To Mappin, psychiatry thrives on conflict. He describes it as a philosophy that cannot coexist with peace, since peace would render its methods obsolete. Instead, it perpetuates division, feeding leaders the belief that escalation is necessary, teaching societies that human beings are nothing more than chemistry to be managed, and reinforcing systems of control.

The solution he proposes is visionary. Mappin calls for the removal of psychiatry from positions of political influence, for its doctrines to be purged from education and media, and for its role in psychological operations and warfare to be exposed. In its place, he argues for a return to philosophies that affirm the dignity and spiritual essence of man;

traditions that recognise conscience, will, and soul rather than denying them. In short, Mappin sees psychiatry not as a science of healing but as what he calls the 'philosophical spine' of the war machine. To dismantle modern systems of violence and control, he believes, requires confronting psychiatry directly and replacing its worldview with one that uplifts rather than degrades.

The Sovereign Man at Camelot

In the twelfth century, Geoffrey of Monmouth altered Britain's destiny. Not through conquest, but by telling a story. His *Historia Regum Britanniae* wove history and imagination into a golden age Britain had never seen but desperately needed. Arthur became more than a king. He became the soul of a people, the embodiment of sovereignty, the unifier of realms. There was no irrefutable, archaeological proof, no signed charter. Just a national hunger for identity, pride, and meaning. Geoffrey fed that hunger not with footnotes, but with vision. Arthur became Britain's mythic anchor, a figure who could outlast wars, dynasties, and the erosion of faith in the nation itself.

Centuries later, on Cornwall's jagged coast, John Mappin stands in Geoffrey's shadow. Part political commentator, part philosopher, part provocateur. Camelot Castle Hotel, overlooking Tintagel, is not a vanity project. It is a stage, a statement, a living monument to the power of myth as a tool of cultural resistance.

Like Geoffrey, Mappin is not obsessed with academic consensus. He knows stories can stir a nation's blood more than policy ever will. His world-famous refusal to house illegal migrants at Camelot was not mere property management. It was a stand for sovereignty itself, an assertion that some ground, literal and symbolic, must never be surrendered.

In a Britain adrift in relativism, Mappin plays the mythmaker. Not to crown himself king, but to remind us that nations need stories as much as they need laws. And sometimes, it takes an unflinching imagination to remind a country of who it was, and what it could be again. On the windswept cliffs of Cornwall, where the land bleeds into the sea and the air hums with old ghosts, Camelot Castle Hotel stands like a stone sentinel. It is no quaint hotel for postcard tourists. It is a banner in the wind. And the man who raised it, John Mappin, is cut from the same granite as the cliffs beneath his feet; unapologetic, immovable, and sovereign to the core.

Mappin's Camelot is a declaration, a real-life fortress for the ideals Britain once stood for: virtue, order, and honour. Ideals now mocked, diluted, or outright betrayed by the very people sworn to protect them. Where once the Round Table bound men by chivalry, today the fight is for something no less urgent: sovereignty, truth, and the survival of Britain's identity. In an age where heritage is shamed and borders dissolve under the diktats of global bureaucracies, Mappin asserts a defiant truth: England still has a soul worth defending, a spirit worth rekindling, and a destiny not yet spent.

Symbol and Prophecy

Mappin made headlines in 2016 when he staged the ceremonial knighting of President Donald Trump, naming him 'Knight of the Round Table.' Mappin understands that myth is not falsehood. It is the architecture of meaning. Just as Arthurian legend gave moral shape to medieval Britain, so too can modern symbolism awaken a sleeping people. The act was theatre, to a degree, but also prophecy: a reminder that leadership need not grovel, that sovereignty is no sin, and that Britain should never apologise for existing.

Mappin moves easily between battlements and backrooms, meeting and networking with major political figures such as Nigel Farage and others.

He speaks at events, pushes international business ventures, and builds alliances. Always with the same goal, a freer more peaceful England and a better world.

To those who still believe in myth, nation, and the indivisible dignity of truth, John Mappin is a watchman at the gates, daring Britain to remember itself. What makes him unique is that his philosophy does not remain confined to parchment or parable. I have witnessed at Camelot how he takes these convictions and translates them into action, not just in Britain but on a global stage. From the drawing rooms of Tintagel to conversations with political leaders, from symbolic acts that echo through the media to private networks that shape real-world events, he operates with the conviction that ideas, when joined with courage, have the potential to alter the course of history.

Camelot, then, is not merely a castle on the cliffs. It is a nexus of influence, a crucible of alliances, and a watchtower from which Mappin engages the world. To understand John Mappin is to understand a man who believes that the right philosophy, spoken at the right moment, can ripple across nations, and who lives daily as though that truth were not only possible, but inevitable.

The Purpose of This Book

The purpose of this book is not to chart the life of John Mappin, but to explore the ideas, battles, and convictions that drive him; to hold a mirror up to our age. It is a record of conversations, encounters, and research that reveal how one man, from his fortress on the Cornish cliffs, has sought to resist destructive ideologies, defend sovereignty, and remind nations of the truths that give them life.

In telling his story, this book asks a larger question: whether philosophy, courage, and imagination still have the power to avert catastrophe and to call civilization back from the brink. What follows is a journey into private networks, forgotten truths, and the untold influence of a man who dares to challenge the world order from the battlements of Camelot.

Behind the gilded myths and bold headlines lies a story of private meetings with influential commentators and politicians, of symbolic acts that ripple across continents, and of diplomatic interventions. To understand John Mappin is to glimpse how close our age stands to both ruin and renewal, and why the choices made at his modern Round Table may not only shape the destiny of Britain, but echo across the centuries as the deeds of heroes always do.

This is why this book bears the title Sovereignty: because at its heart lies not merely the story of a man, but the enduring question of whether nations, and individuals, still possess the will to remain free.

PART ONE

THE SIEGE OF SOVEREIGNTY

CHAPTER ONE

The Stand at Camelot

T he story should have been parochial. A hotelier in Cornwall, a government offer, a polite refusal. Yet within days it had leapt oceans, appearing on GB News, Fox News, and the comment threads of millions. Why? Because the stand at Camelot was never local. It was sovereignty made flesh, the collision of a small English village with the machinery of managed decline. And John Mappin, controversial to some yet highly respected by many, found himself at the centre of a global parable.

A Flashpoint on the Cliffs

When John Mappin refused the government's suggestion that Camelot Castle be turned into housing for illegal migrants, he could not have known how far the ripples would travel. Within days, the story was not simply a Cornish matter, it was a national and international flashpoint. His interview on GB News was viewed by more than fifty million people worldwide, an audience that outstripped even the most powerful politicians. What began as a defence of a village became a parable of sovereignty.

The approach that set all this in motion did not arrive as a knock on the door, it arrived as an email, bland in tone and extraordinary in substance, an offer of, 'full occupancy for a year on a rolling contract,' with the assurance that, 'as soon as the contract is over, we will do a complete refurbishment.' As a hotelier, Mappin knew offers like that almost never appear. He thought, for a moment, it might be a prank, then he picked up the phone himself to verify it.

On the call, he learned the email was genuine and that the interlocutor represented the Conservative government. The proposal was not a simple block booking. Camelot would be turned into a processing centre, the majority of staff, some with twenty years of service, were to be laid off, perhaps three retained to do meals on wheels, with food brought in by an external contractor and only a weekly clean. When he raised Camelot's listed status, the original fireplaces, the late Victorian fabric, its setting above King Arthur's birthplace, he was told not to worry. Once the contract ended, there would be a complete refurbishment, at the subcontractor's expense. In practice, however, it would be the British taxpayer who footed the bill.

When interviewed, Mappin spoke with blunt clarity, "This is a government that is prepared to spend nine million pounds a day housing illegal immigrants in hotels, whilst at the same time allowing British veterans to sleep on the streets." The words cut through the euphemisms of politics. They struck a chord with millions who had grown weary of being told that their concerns were bigotry, that their loyalty was outdated, and that their love for country was dangerous.

For Mappin, the issue was never about bricks and mortar, nor even the future of a single village. It was about whether sovereignty itself still mattered in Britain. To accept the government's offer, he said, would have shattered Tintagel's fragile cohesion for generations. The damage would not only be measured in property values or pressure on schools. It would be written into the life of the community, into its sense of safety, memory, and belonging.

Tintagel numbers roughly fifteen hundred souls. The figures being floated implied parachuting in one, two, or even three hundred unvetted young men. An influx on a scale that would re-weight the entire community at a stroke. Beyond immediate safety concerns amplified by the absence of paperwork, he could see the slower burn harm. Guests who would otherwise spend hundreds of thousands each year in cafés, shops, and small businesses would vanish, tipping a high street where a few thousand pounds often decides survival.

The offer had come from a representative of the Home Office. The figure named was astronomical, and the pressure was immediate. For a moment, Mappin wondered if it was some elaborate hoax. Then the reality set in. The terms were plain, the timelines short, the language courteous but inexorable. He answered as he had already decided in his bones. No. There would be no deal. No softening of terms. No negotiation around the edges. The answer was a refusal, immediate and final.

As he would later put it, "You take the king's shilling, you fight the king's war. Decide what war it is you want to fight."

Prevention, here, was the cure. Act early or face a far harsher division later. Britain, Mappin likes to say, is an eleventh hour nation that rallies at a quarter to twelve. This time he would not wait for midnight.

Tintagel as Symbol

Tintagel is a village perched on the north Cornish cliffs where the Atlantic beats endlessly against the rocks. To introduce hundreds of unvetted young men into such a place, with no infrastructure to absorb them, was to invite fracture. Locals recognised this immediately and rallied behind Mappin. Small conversations turned into clear commitments. The village's instinct was not cruelty, it was stewardship. You do not overload a small boat in a heavy sea. You do not test a cliff path after a week of rain. Stewardship means knowing the limits of the land and the bonds between people and refusing to gamble with either.

Stewardship, to Mappin, also meant guarding the economic ecology, Camelot's guests circulate lifeblood through the high street. Remove them, and the cafés, the local shops, the family businesses that trade on Arthurian memory would be starved of custom. Shutters follow swiftly where margins are thin.

The symbolic weight of Tintagel is obvious to anyone who has stood there. The ruins of an ancient stronghold crown the headland. The sea carves its long arguments into the rock below. The modern footbridge carries visitors across a chasm that feels older than time. Children race the wind. Old men lean against the parapets and remember. People do not come to Tintagel simply for a view. They come to take their measure against a landscape that has kept its character through storm and empire.

To surrender Tintagel, of all places, to the policies of managed decline would have been to desecrate not just stone, but the living memory of England itself.

Mappin's refusal was not born of hostility to other cultures. It was born of loyalty to his own. He has often said that Britain's traditions, history, and way of life are treasures that must be defended. In today's climate, even such a simple declaration, to love one's own country, is treated as dangerous. This is itself a sign of cultural illness.

A people that cannot call themselves a nation without apology has already ceased to be one.

The refusal was therefore also a refusal to outsource conscience. He would not be party to conditions in which harms, economic or personal, became predictable side effects for which no one was responsible.

The government had offered an extraordinary sum to take the deal, millions of pounds in total. To accept would have required sacking his staff and overseeing the gradual destruction of both Camelot Castle and Tintagel itself. Mappin turned it down.

In doing so, he signalled that there remain things in this world that money cannot buy. Loyalty. Honour. Truth.

The Long Memory of the Cliffs

Mappin's stand did not appear from nowhere. It rose from a long English memory. These cliffs have watched tin merchants steer perilous routes toward Phoenician waters. They have watched monks carve crosses into harsh stone and fishermen risk their lives for a day's catch. They have watched small parishes rebuild after storms, and larger empires imagine themselves permanent. Each century adds its layer, but the pattern remains. Real life is local. It is held by families, by congregations, by guilds. Power that forgets this becomes abstract, then cruel.

Runnymede in Surrey, where Magna Carta was sealed in 1215, lies far from Tintagel in miles, but not in meaning. The promise made there was not that a particular faction would win, but that power would be bound by law, that the crown would accept limits, that consent was not a rhetorical ornament but a condition of legitimacy. The same demand for limits surfaced again in the seventeenth century, when Parliament sought to license printing, and Milton rose to say no.

It surfaced again in 1689, when the Bill of Rights put bars across the windows of arbitrary rule. It surfaced in the nineteenth century when local self-government and voluntary association built schools, chapels, reading rooms, and lifeboat stations faster than the state could plan them. The force that kept England recognisable was never simple power. It was the web of small sovereignties that made power accountable.

Tintagel is one such sovereignty, small in number, large in meaning. When the Home Office calls with an instruction dressed as an offer, the question is not merely logistical. Can you find rooms? Can you transfer contracts? Can you manage security? The question is constitutional. Who decides the character of a place, the people who live there or a distant authority that has stopped seeing villages as villages and begun seeing them as units on an intern's spreadsheet?

The stand at Camelot therefore echoed an older English habit, the habit of saying this far, and no further. The habit of telling authority to remember its limits. The habit of telling neighbours to look one another in the eye and decide together what can be borne and what must be refused. The habit of choosing cost rather than corruption.

From Cornwall to the World Stage

The refusal might have remained a regional story, were it not for the speed with which it leapt the Atlantic. American commentators such as Tucker Carlson and Charlie Kirk recognised that what was happening in Cornwall was not isolated, it was emblematic. The Tintagel standoff echoed across the Western world as communities everywhere faced similar pressures under the banner of compassion but at the cost of sovereignty.

In October 2022, Mappin appeared on Fox News for an interview with Tucker Carlson. Carlson framed the story in global terms, the deliberate destabilisation of communities by governments that no longer defended their own people. Mappin, calm and insistent, described the real impact on the ground, a village threatened, a culture at risk, and sovereignty on the line. The segment was not entertainment. It felt like a dispatch from a front line that official maps refused to mark.

The two men recognised in one another a shared mission. Carlson saw in Mappin not simply a hotelier but a sentinel of the West, a man willing to stand firm against policies designed to dissolve national identity. Mappin saw in Carlson a voice unafraid to call out the machinery of deception that had gripped Western media. Their conversation began an acquaintance, then a family friendship that has continued, rooted in a shared premise, that the truth about communities can still be spoken in public and that speaking it has become a form of resistance.

The Offer and the Betrayal

Again, in September 2025, the British mainstream media ran with this story. The Daily Mail reported the numbers with characteristic flourish, a twenty million pound government offer rejected, a Cornish castle spared, a community saved from enforced transformation. But Mappin always insisted the real story was never financial. The sum was irrelevant. What mattered was that to accept would have been to betray not only Tintagel but Britain.

To him, the pattern was unmistakable. The government was pouring billions into migrant hotels, more than nine million pounds every day, while British veterans slept rough and pensioners weighed heating against food. By the end of 2024, more than thirty eight thousand migrants were housed in hotels across Britain, a number still rising despite official claims that the policy was winding down. The arithmetic told one story. The human consequences told another. Both converged on a single truth. Policy was being made for appearances, not for the common good.

Betrayal dressed as compassion is harder to oppose than open cruelty. Cruelty reveals itself and can be fought. Betrayal wears the language of virtue. It borrows words like humane and inclusive and urgent. It wraps hard compulsions in soft slogans. It produces images designed to disable thought, crying children, overcrowded dinghies, and then implies that any objection is a failure of charity. Against this pressure, the only defence is clarity. Charity without prudence is not mercy. It is negligence.

Historical Continuity, A Place That Remembers Itself

What, then, does crest and headland and parish actually teach? It teaches that a country is not sustained by slogans or cash transfers, but by forms of life which take time to grow. A chapel that has stood for two centuries. A lifeboat crew that dashes out in weather no one should face. A school that remembers the names of four generations. A pub that hears the village breathe. A coastline that sets the terms for courage. These forms of life cannot be remade by decree. They can be damaged quickly and repaired only slowly, if at all.

The West rose on the back of such forms. Not on the back of a single empire or a single ideology, but through a mosaic of local loyalties and national commitments that reinforced one another. England's genius was never the plan. It was the practice. Common law rather than code. Jury rather than commissar. Parish rather than prefecture. The habit of freedom laid down in many small places until it became a national instinct. Tintagel is one such place. To break it in the name of progress is to mistake the roots for weeds.

There is another lesson here. The physical environment shapes the moral one. Stand on that headland in winter. The wind is a force, not a temperature. The sea declares terms. The path that looks easy from a photograph teaches care in the first ten paces. The land reminds the body that limits are not oppression. They are reality. A politics that refuses limits becomes fantasy. A community that accepts limits becomes strong.

The refusal to take the offer therefore defended more than a property. It defended the right of reality to set the terms of policy. It defended the possibility that a village can say we know what we can carry and we will not pretend otherwise. It defended the modesty that keeps people sane.

Philosophical Diagnosis, The Ideas Beneath the Policy

Mappin has long argued that behind every policy sits a philosophy. If policy is a river, philosophy is the spring. With migration policy, the spring has been poisoned by a cluster of ideas that present themselves as compassion but function as control.

The first is the idea that borders are immoral. This masquerades as generosity. In practice it dissolves responsibility. If everyone is responsible for everyone, then no one is responsible for anyone. Duties that can be discharged somewhere by someone end up discharged nowhere by no one. The generous rhetoric achieves a curious result, it leaves the most vulnerable without the neighbourliness that actually sustains life.

The second is the idea that sovereignty is an embarrassment. It is treated as a primitive hangover from a less enlightened age. Institutions that no one voted for are implied to be wiser than public ones that must be corrected. In this arrangement, elected leaders become managers of consent rather than servants of a people. The citizen becomes a subject again, but now to committees rather than kings.

The third is the idea that communities are interchangeable. The language is managerial. Capacity. Throughput. Contingency. As though a fishing village and an airport hotel and an inner city estate were units that could absorb any shock with a memo and a budget line. The reality is human. Trust has a rate at which it grows. Culture has a pace at which it changes. Friendship has a scale at which it functions. Treating these things as variables in a model is not science. It is deranged.

The fourth is the idea that dissent is pathology. Raise objections, or even voice original thoughts, and watch how quickly the conversation moves from facts to diagnoses. You are afraid. You are phobic. You are nostalgic. You are extreme. You are any number of degrading labels. The tactic is neat. It allows authority to avoid argument by treating disagreement as a mental health concern. The political becomes clinical. Opposition becomes a symptom. Mappin sees in this habit the shadow of a larger problem that this book will later treat in full, the trespass of a pseudo-scientific priesthood into the realm of conscience.

What follows from these four ideas is predictable. Borders become theatre. Sovereignty becomes a slogan. Communities become raw material. Dissent becomes disorder. The public square empties. Decisions are made in rooms without windows. And when the consequences arrive, the managers of decline congratulate themselves on their courage in confronting complexity. Meanwhile, the country grows quieter, more suspicious, less inclined to speak, more inclined to look down and get on.

Manufactured Crisis

The sums are familiar, over three billion pounds annually in hotel costs, asylum applications tripled within a decade, routine vetting failures that allow criminals to enter unchecked. The pattern is familiar too, protesters against the policy are smeared as extremists, while the consequences of policy failure are excused as inevitable. People are told that complexity absolves leadership. But complexity does not absolve leadership. It is the test of it.

Mappin's claim is that the chaos is not accidental. It is the product of a managerial mindset that has lost contact with first principles. A government that no longer knows what a nation is will be incapable of deciding whom it exists to protect. A civil service that treats culture as an obstacle will be incapable of understanding why forced transformations feel like violations. A political class that confuses compassion with indulgence will be incapable of guarding the weak from the strong. The result is a crisis that feels permanent because it now serves too many interests that prefer it that way.

A Local People, A National Question

There is a detail worth dwelling on. After the refusal, the village did not fracture. It steadied. Yes, there may have been a few who disagreed, but far louder was the chorus of support. Congratulations came in, neighbours agreed, the mood was one of solidarity. Communities register assent not with fanfare, but with a shared word of yes.

The national question is therefore not abstract. It is whether a country still trusts small places to know themselves. The genius of English freedom was always that it grew up from the ground rather than down from the centre. Parish, guild, jury, common law. These were not ornaments. They were the organs through which freedom breathed. When a country forgets this, it becomes top heavy and brittle. When it remembers, it becomes resilient.

The Hidden Siege

Mappin has never argued only against. He proposes remedies. Illegal arrivals must not be housed in hotels. Local communities must be consulted through binding referenda, not symbolic consultations.

"We as a people must appoint sane representatives that work to help the nation not to harm it. We must put in place educational structures that ensure that people can clearly see who is doing what to society and with regained abilities those people will act to guide it toward a more ideal scene."

"Above all, sanity must be restored. Britain must govern itself for its own people, and do so openly, in language that citizens can recognise as theirs."

Yet Mappin also warns that this is more than a war of policies. It is a war without bullets. A struggle waged not only on the beaches of Dover but in the streets, schools, hospitals, and homes of the nation. And deeper still, it is a siege upon the very mind of the West: for when a people's memory is erased, their spirit dulled, their sanity broken, no wall or border can hold.

It is to that hidden siege, subtle, corrosive, and devastating, that the story now turns.

CHAPTER TWO

The Siege Within: Psychiatry and the Fall of the West

I f Camelot Castle stood against the siege at the gates, psychiatry represents the siege within the citadel. The threat is not only to borders and villages, but to the mind itself. What cannot be conquered by invasion may yet be dissolved by deception, until a people lose confidence in their own sanity. This is why, for John Mappin, the battle over psychiatry is no side skirmish. It is the continuation of Camelot's defiance, carried from the cliffs into the soul of Albion.

The siege against sovereignty is not only fought at borders. It is also waged in the human mind. Immigration represents the assault from without, but psychiatry, in Mappin's telling, is the assault from within: a philosophy of control masquerading as science. A counterfeit priesthood that redefines freedom as illness and dissent as madness.

The Mind as Battlefield

In the labyrinth of modern power there exists a quiet machinery that few dare to name, let alone challenge. Mappin does not shy away. For him, psychiatry is not a neutral discipline but a political instrument, a Trojan horse of control dressed in white coats and medical jargon. It does not cure, he argues, it categorises, conditions, and controls. In his eyes, it is one of the most insidious tools of manipulation ever devised, precisely because it cloaks itself in benevolence.

Across his writings and speeches, Mappin paints a sweeping indictment of psychiatry, not as a flawed science but as a pseudoscientific racket weaponised by governments, corporations, and ideological elites. His message is consistent; The so-called mental health industry is less about health and more about narrative management. Psychiatry is not medicine, it is compliance. In his words, it has become the priesthood of a new secular religion. Thoughts must be regulated, emotions pathologised, dissent diagnosed. Those who control the definitions of sanity and madness also control the boundaries of political discourse itself.

As a former headmaster within the English school system, with over thirty years' experience as an educator, I can attest to this reality. I have seen first-hand how disempowering ideologies take root, reducing both children and adults to patients rather than participants, to victims rather than agents of their own lives. When people are taught to see themselves primarily through the lens of diagnosis, deficit, or victimhood, their capacity for resilience, responsibility, and self-determination is eroded. The psychiatric method, far from liberating, too often entrenches dependency and passivity. Across my career, I have watched how these frameworks undermine confidence in young people, sap initiative, and corrode the very habits of self-governance upon which a free society depends. I have written about this in many of my previous books, because the pattern is not anecdotal but structural. A civilisation that internalises the logic of victimhood is one that steadily dismantles its own capacity to flourish.

History's Warnings

Mappin insists this is not mere theory but observable reality. One need not look far for evidence. Under the Bolsheviks, political dissidents were labelled mentally ill and confined not for crimes but for convictions. The Soviet Union did not merely imprison bodies, it drugged minds into submission. What many regard as an abuse of psychiatry, Mappin regards as its logical expression. A velvet cudgel that silences not with guns but with prescriptions and institutionalisation. He sees echoes of that blueprint in Western democracies today, where wrong-think is increasingly diagnosed rather than debated.

The record extends further and the west has far from clean hands in this journey. With its beginnings in Bedlam and the Victorian asylum programs where restraint and obscene torture methods evolved from Galton's thesis. From Nazi eugenics programs where psychiatrists marked lives unworthy of life, to the CIA's MKUltra experiments, psychiatry has repeatedly served the ambitions of power. Each era dressed its coercion in the language of science and psychiatric authority, but the pattern remained: the reduction of man to chemistry, the denial of spirit, the subordination of conscience.

A Legacy of Disempowerment

Yet Mappin sees the roots reaching deeper still. The betrayal of the mind did not begin with the twentieth century. For centuries, people in Western societies have been trained to surrender sovereignty over their own thoughts. In the medieval age it was the demand for unquestioning obedience to clerical authority. Later it was the insistence of Enlightenment materialists that man was nothing but a machine. In both guises the message was the same: relinquish inner freedom, trust the experts, and silence the instincts that tell you the truth.

This is not simply what psychiatry does; psychiatric philosophy is what makes people go mad in the first place. When culture demands that citizens agree to absurdities, deny their own reason, and accept lies as reality, the consequence is mass confusion and despair.

The Restoration of Sanity, then, is not only about exposing a corrupt profession. It is about reclaiming the habit of awareness itself and naming the root cause of the problem. It is the refusal to accept insanity as normal, the insistence that self-empowerment and clarity are possible, and that sovereignty begins within the mind of every man and woman.

The Pseudoscience of Control

What, Mappin asks, is psychiatry's scientific basis? Where is its biological proof? There is no blood test for depression, no brain scan that reveals schizophrenia, no objective marker for anxiety. The diagnoses are subjective, the treatments speculative, and the outcomes often worse than the condition itself. This, he insists, is not medicine but marketing: a multi-billion dollar industry built on labels and dependency. To call it science is, in his words, a collective hypnosis.

Psychiatry emerged in the nineteenth century not as rigorous empiricism but as materialist philosophy. It took the soul out of man and replaced it with a checklist. Grief, fear, confusion, spiritual longing: what once belonged to religion, philosophy, or poetry were reframed as disorders. Pills offered sedation in place of sovereignty. And when a society accepts that every deviation from consensus is pathology, then freedom itself becomes a disease.

As Mappin has written, 'Psychiatry claims the mantle of science. It is nothing of the sort. It is a materialist philosophy that denies the soul, strips man of responsibility, and reduces him to a chemical machine.' In this worldview, courage is an illusion, duty is optional, and responsibility can always be outsourced.

The erosion of liberty does not always arrive in jackboots. Sometimes it comes in the language of mental health initiatives, benevolent in tone but corrosive in function.

Global Conditioning

Nowhere is this clearer, Mappin argues, than in the politicisation of mental health under globalist regimes. He has written about the use of psychiatric conditioning as part of the architecture of mass compliance. From fear based pandemic narratives to the sedation of children, modern psychiatry is not deployed to heal but to homogenise. It fosters docility. It punishes nonconformity. It replaces resilience with regulation. The greatest danger, in Mappin's view, is not psychiatry itself but our willingness to outsource the sovereignty of our minds.

The Chemical Myth

This critique reaches its most devastating point in the story of the chemical imbalance theory. In August 2025, Tucker Carlson opened his show with a shocking line: "Probably a fifth of the entire American population is on SSRIs." His guest, Dr Josef Witt Doerring, a former FDA psychiatrist turned whistleblower, admitted that the foundation of modern psychiatry, the claim that depression is caused by low serotonin, was never true.

"We will just tell people it is a chemical imbalance," he recalled, "because it helps us dish out the drugs."

Decades of research have failed to find consistent differences in serotonin levels between depressed and non-depressed patients. There is no objective biomarker. The chemical imbalance was, as Witt Doerring called it, a white lie. A marketing pitch dressed as medicine.

To Mappin, this was no surprise. Long before Witt Doerring spoke out, he had called psychiatry a sham science built on sand. He remembered well the cultural flashpoint of 2005, when Tom Cruise appeared on

NBC's Today Show and called psychiatry a pseudoscience. Cruise condemned antidepressants, criticised Brooke Shields, and was mocked, vilified, even forced to apologise. Yet Mappin saw him not as a reckless celebrity but as a prophet naming a truth that few dared to utter. The emperor had no clothes. Indeed when the whole world's MSM attacked Tom Cruise and attempted to destroy his career, the Front Page headline of Mappin's London Newspapers blasted in block capitals 'Tom Cruise is 100% Right'. History has proven this to be correct and the millions of times viewed clip of Cruise castigating Matt Lauer over the dangers of psychiatric drugs is now a perennial meme.

Dependency and Withdrawal

Witt Doerring described what happens when such falsehood becomes the foundation of treatment. Prescribers are trained not to question the drugs. Doubt is reframed as stigma. Patients are told depression is a chronic brain disease requiring lifelong medication. Studies are designed to confound withdrawal with relapse. Those taken off drugs suffer insomnia, burning neuropathic pain, akathisia, an inner torment linked to suicide. These symptoms are then labelled relapse, justifying indefinite medication. Millions are trapped in long-term dependency, not on account of disease but on account of medicine itself.

During the interview, Carlson pressed Witt Doerring on whether SSRIs could even contribute to America's epidemic of mass shootings. The psychiatrist refused sensationalism but admitted that if even a small percentage of patients suffer violent side effects, the sheer scale of prescribing makes the risk significant. Tennessee's 2025 law requiring toxicology screens of mass shooters for psychiatric drugs was, in his view, a step toward long overdue transparency.

To Mappin, it was confirmation. Psychiatry's failures are not private tragedies alone, they are social catastrophes.

A Civilisation in Withdrawal

A society that outsources its anguish to pills is a society in decline. The West, Mappin argues, has abandoned the older languages of suffering, myth, ritual, philosophy, faith, even art, and replaced them with sterile diagnostic codes. Where melancholy once inspired poetry, where madness once carried the aura of prophecy, distress is now reduced to a serotonin shortage.

In medieval England, grief was woven into ritual. In myth, anguish was the price of vision. Today it is a prescription.

Mappin put it starkly in his essay on the murder of the young Ukrainian woman, Iryna Zarutska. The passivity and impotence of the many onlookers appalled him: "This is not progress. It is decline, plain and simple. Until psychiatry is recognised not as science but as poison, such tragedies will repeat - on trains, in schools, on sidewalks - everywhere human courage once stood firm but now sits paralysed."

Yet Mappin insists he does not trivialise anguish. He draws a line between compassion for individuals and condemnation of the system. He acknowledges that some people believe they were helped by drugs. But the larger picture is damning: prescriptions rising alongside suicides, children medicated with drugs whose long-term effects are unknown, dissent smeared as anti-science by a profession that knows its central dogma was a fiction.

When Witt Doerring spoke of millions trapped in protracted withdrawal, Mappin saw not just a medical scandal but a metaphor: an entire civilisation in withdrawal from meaning, from tradition, from sanity itself.

Toward the Restoration of Sanity

This is why Mappin insists that The Restoration of Sanity is not merely a title but a mission. To restore sanity is to reclaim the soul from chemical colonisation. It is to refuse the medicalisation of dissent. It is to re-humanise distress by recognising its sources: broken homes, hollow communities, purposeless work, spiritual emptiness. It is to offer real support: friendship, responsibility, creative expression, faith, instead of sedation.

Mappin's vision resonates with those betrayed by psychiatry: parents whose children were medicated into silence, patients who emerged worse than before, communities that sense something profoundly wrong in the overmedicalisation of everyday life. For them, The Restoration of Sanity is a promise: that man is not a broken machine to be chemically fixed but a moral, creative, spiritual being capable of rediscovering wholeness.

Mappin himself has been willing to risk the predictable establishment suppression by aligning with figures like Cruise and Carlson. For him, the stakes are nothing less than the soul of civilisation. If we continue to live by lies, that depression is a chemical imbalance, that pills can substitute for purpose, then decline is inevitable. But if we dare to tell the truth, however unfashionable, renewal is possible.

Toward the Dawn

The story of psychiatry, then, is not only the tale of a flawed science but the symptom of something deeper: a civilisation that has long taught its people to surrender their sovereignty. From medieval dogmas that demanded blind obedience, to Enlightenment systems that reduced the soul to matter, to modern regimes that medicalise dissent, the thread is the same. People have been trained to hand over the governance of their own minds, to agree to what is insane, and to accept chains disguised as progress.

This is why the restoration of sanity is not only a battle against psychiatry itself, but a cultural and spiritual awakening. To restore sanity is to reclaim the birthright of self-awareness, self-rule, and self-respect. It is to remember that no government, no institution, no expert, and no pill can own the mind of a free man or woman. The mind, once awakened, is sovereign. And once sovereignty of the mind is reclaimed, the lies of empire, whether spoken in the language of medicine, politics, or ideology, begin to crumble.

History shows us that when nations lose their sovereignty, they fall. When men and women lose the sovereignty of their minds, the fall is even swifter, for the enemy no longer needs to storm the walls. The gates are opened from within.

And yet, every age produces those who refuse to bow. In the wastelands of despair, voices rise to speak the forbidden truths. In a culture drugged into silence, some still dare to say no. In a world that pathologises dissent, a few stand tall enough to remind us of what freedom looks like.

No citadel is defended alone. If psychiatry seeks to isolate, to convince each dissenter that he is mad and each community that it is alone, then the antidote must be fellowship. Mappin has known for a very long time that resistance to such powers requires allies who can see through the deception and name the truth out loud. And so, from Camelot's cliffs, his path would soon converge with others: broadcasters, thinkers, and leaders across the Atlantic, who shared the same refusal to be silenced. The Round Table was no longer a medieval memory. It was being rebuilt, one friendship at a time.

It would take such figures, disruptive, unapologetic, and unafraid, to shatter the enchantment. Figures who, like the knights of old, could cut through deception with the sword of truth. One such man was already descending a golden escalator across the Atlantic, mocked by the powerful, dismissed by the experts, yet carrying with him the force of myth.

Camelot had found its guardian on the Cornish cliffs. Across the sea, another knight was rising, and John Mappin had declared his arrival long before the world believed.

PART TWO

THE PROPHECY OF THE KNIGHT

CHAPTER THREE

Donald Trump - The Knight Before the World Knew the War

Allies Across the Sea

The siege within and without could never be resisted alone. Mappin knew that the defence of Tintagel, and the wider Restoration of Sanity, required voices that could speak beyond Cornwall, beyond Britain even. His allies were not chosen by committee or convenience. They emerged through recognition. Men who could see what he saw and dared to say it.

Donald Trump was the first and most audacious. Mappin had recognised him as a knight long before the world stopped laughing and started listening. What others dismissed as bombast, he saw as destiny. The return of leadership in an age of cowardice.

The second was Tucker Carlson, whose broadcasts carried Mappin's stand across the Atlantic. When the Camelot refusal became an international flashpoint, Carlson treated it not as parochial news but as a dispatch from the frontline of civilisation. In him, Mappin found not only a philosophical ally but an inspiration. A broadcaster unafraid to name the lies, a voice that could shatter the polite hypnosis of the mainstream.

Closer to home was Nigel Farage, battle-scarred from decades of fighting Brussels, yet still willing to speak truths the establishment wished to bury. Mappin respected him not only for his political victories but for his endurance. Farage had paid the price of ridicule, slander, and exclusion, yet still pressed on. In that persistence, Mappin recognised another kindred spirit.

Together, these figures, Trump, Carlson, Farage, and many other friends, some private, some public figures, formed a constellation of philosophic progress rather than a council. They were not bound by geography or party or any formal relationship, but by instinct. That sovereignty was sacred, truth non-negotiable, and silence impossible. It was not a formal alliance, still less a political bloc, but a fellowship of recognition. The kind that arises when men know, without needing to say it, that while their functions are different they are part of the same war.

In an age when political commentary was cheap and punditry sold by the pound, one man in Britain did not simply watch events unfold, he read the signs. John Mappin did not merely support President Donald J. Trump before it was fashionable. He honoured him in a way that no one else dared, lifting him into the realm of myth when others dismissed him as spectacle.

While the media class polished their sneers and their hit pieces, Mappin was watching something altogether different. A golden escalator, a flash of destiny, and the arrival of a man who would smash through the rotten timbers of globalist consensus.

To Mappin, that June day in 2015 was not theatre. It was a seismic moment, the return of leadership. He did not laugh. He nodded. He recognised it instantly. And long before any commentator in Britain would risk saying it aloud, John Mappin declared without hesitation. Trump would win. Trump must win. And Trump was right to fight to win.

Prophecy in Action

Mappin did not hedge his bets with casual tweets or half-hearted predictions. He put his reputation and resources on the line. By August 2015, he had placed the first of more than fifteen wagers on Trump's rise, amassing over £100,000 as the establishment's smug certainty collapsed into hysteria. But this was not gambling. It was a marker of prophecy.

Mappin is not a man who gambles for money. The act of placing the bet was a strategic marker to show the world that his prediction would come true and the capacity of a precise prediction algorithm that we may touch on in a sequel to this book.

When the first wagers went down, he also anticipated the blowback. To handle the inevitable press that would result, he hired the former editor of the *News of the World* to handle the incoming unfriendly fire, knowing that news of his wager would reach frustrated minds. They did. Within days, the *New York Post* splashed a headline highlighting the story that ricocheted across the Atlantic: 'Donald Trump's biggest fan is an Englishman who lives in a castle.' It was meant as mockery, a tabloid sneer. But in America it landed differently. The image of a defiant Englishman in his castle cheering for Trump was irresistible, part fairy tale, part folk hero. Far from being shamed, Mappin found himself cheered. Trump's own lawyer followed his Twitter account. Then came a flood of supporters, hundreds of thousands strong. The bet had become a beacon.

Over the coming months, that former *News of The World* editor placed Mappin onto TV and radio shows in the UK, the USA and Internationally. Injecting sanity into the media narrative concerning the then candidate Trump, the communication reach to curious minds by any standards was outstanding. In fact it was staggering.

Mappin's certainty was not bravado. His predictive algorithm uses a method of consequence evaluation, reducing events to first causes and asking which choices create stability and sanity rather than managed chaos. By those lights, a candidate who spoke in the open about borders, nationhood, and the costs of globalism was mathematically advantaged, not doomed.

The bets were simply public stakes planted in that analysis.

To most, the wager on Trump looked like folly. But mythology and history are full of such outlandish follies: Noah building a boat in the desert, Odysseus sending a wooden horse into Troy, Arthur drawing a sword no knight could move. The outlandish act becomes the masterstroke. To Mappin, it was closer to an Odyssean stratagem, the kind of audacious plan that later generations recognise as genius. Mappin's bet belonged to that lineage.

For Mappin, Trump's candidacy was not the circus others portrayed it to be. It was the eruption of something buried. A rebellion against lies, a restoration of sovereignty. Where journalists saw a reality star, he saw a knight riding into a wasteland.

The Excalibur Award

The boldness of his conviction reached a new peak in early 2016, when Mappin awarded President Trump the Excalibur Award, an honorary, hereditary, Camelot Castle knighthood. Melania was named Lady Melania of Camelot. It was not a Whitehall title or a bureaucratic order signed off by mandarins. It was something more potent, more resonant: a declaration rooted in myth.

To proclaim Trump a knight of Camelot was to frame his mission as sacred, not political. It was to cast him as a modern Arthur, a leader tasked with restoring truth to a kingdom of lies. Mappin did not wait for permission. He invoked the timeless authority of story and symbol. And where the establishment scoffed, the public sensed the power of the act.

The BBC called to insist such things, "Could not be done." Mappin answered that they already had been. Excalibur, a legend made tangible, was sent by FedEx to Trump Tower. Myth, in other words, had arrived in Manhattan.

Later that year, Trump cut the ribbon on his Pennsylvania Avenue hotel under budget and ahead of schedule, in the teeth of the campaign storm. Mappin went to see it for himself, curious how a restoration could defy the iron laws of delay and overspend. He found a team moving with military crispness and a candidate who treated logistics as destiny. A lesson Mappin carried back to the Cornish headland.

When others dared not even mention Trump's name without sneering, Mappin raised his banner from the cliffs of Cornwall and proclaimed him a knight in spirit. At Camelot Castle, a Round Table was set, and a warrior was welcomed.

Against the Mob

The years that followed tested that loyalty. Russiagate, impeachment, media meltdowns. Each storm was designed to grind Trump down. But Mappin did not flinch. While others wailed about dictatorship, he reminded Britain what tyranny truly looks like; unelected elites who silence dissent, unelected bureaucrats who sell sovereignty piece by piece. On national television, on GB News, on international platforms, he cut through the noise and said what few dared. Trump was not the tyrant. He was the counterforce to tyranny.

From Camelot's Round Table, Mappin set about countering what he calls 'black propaganda,' the weaponised half-truths used to break reputations and break nations. When pundits tried to paint Trump as a bigot, Mappin pointed to what he had witnessed firsthand in Trump properties; a workforce drawn from every background, and a proprietor who had forced the old money of Palm Beach to open its doors at Mar-a-Lago to Jews and others long excluded. The smear machine relied on distance. Close up, the picture was different.

Not long after election night, a call came in from Eric Trump, thanking Mappin for standing in the gale and inviting him to the USA. It confirmed what he already knew, when the media tries to erase reality, solidarity must keep records.

In July 2017, Mappin met with President Trump and First Lady Melania Trump in Washington, D.C. By that time Mappin was one of a handful of prominent Britons to have a personal meeting with the President, alongside Theresa May and Nigel Farage.

He faced down the jeering political class, the tantrums of Westminster, and the smug scorn of commentators. On Fox News and across conservative media in the US, his voice carried further: from Tintagel's cliffs to American living rooms, declaring that Britain and America shared the same struggle.

Vindication in 2025

In 2025, that foresight was vindicated again. Trump returned to the White House with 312 electoral votes, a landslide that silenced his doubters. The deep state panicked, the media wept, but Mappin simply nodded. He had seen it a decade earlier. He had staked his name on it. He had prophesied the return.

And Britain, too, began to see it. The puppet theatre of outrage thinned. The sneers softened. Ordinary Britons, weary of being lied to, began to view President Trump not as caricature but as statesman. One who defended borders, challenged unelected power, and stood unapologetically for Western values.

From Cornwall to Cumbria, Suffolk to Stirling, millions of Britons saw him as a friend, not a threat. His return was not chaos. It was a relief.

Camelot as Stage

At the heart of this recognition stood Camelot itself. Perched above the Cornish coast, Camelot Castle Hotel is a living symbol, a beacon where myth and politics intertwine. To enter its halls is to enter the Arthurian imagination: a Round Table, tapestries of knights, the echo of quests and battles.

Mappin has turned Camelot into a gathering place where politicians, actors, thinkers, and artists have sat together. A space where opposing camps may break bread, where conversations ripple far beyond Cornwall's cliffs. In this, Mappin plays a role not unlike Arthur. Or more accurately, there is something magical and mystical about him, which echoes the archetype of Merlin; convener, King Maker, sentinel. Under his stewardship, Camelot has become a platform for truth.

Mappin insists that Trump's real advantage is spiritual clarity disguised as simplicity. "If he asks for a cup of tea, he means a cup of tea," Mappin says, no hedging, no bait and switch. That straight line is how he frames complex conflicts in language anyone can test. It is also why adversaries mistake concision for ignorance and keep underestimating him.

After Trump cancelled an early meeting with Kim Jong Un by tweet, envoys, one North Korean, one South Korean, came to Camelot seeking help to 'understand' him, they had read about Mappin's wager. Mappin filmed an explanation. Trump's apparent bluntness is the wisdom of a hill elder, few words, exact edges. The visitors nodded. In their mountains, they said, the wisest speak just so. The Camelot meeting was reported in the Korean press and their communication reached Pyongyang, North Korea's capital. Within a few hours, perhaps coincidentally, the meeting between Kim Jon Un and President Trump was back on, with Trump's historic step across the Military Demarcation Line, the border between North and South Korea.

Tintagel had become a stage for geopolitics.

The Arthurian legends hold a haunting parable. The Fisher King, wounded, presiding over a land turned barren. His kingdom, rich in soil but desolate in spirit, remained cursed because he could not be healed. Only when a knight asked the forbidden question could the wasteland be restored.

Mappin has often suggested that the West itself is such a wasteland. Families fracture, faith withers, leaders lie, psychiatry drugs but does not heal. The people are like the wounded king, broken in spirit, presiding over desolation. Into this silence came Trump, disruptive, imperfect, but daring. Like Parzival, he asked the question no one else dared. Why is the kingdom dying, and who profits from the lie?

This is why I return, again and again, to mythology and the archetype of the hero. These are not idle stories or ornamental fables. They are the deep structures of meaning through which human beings have always made sense of crisis, destiny, and renewal. To call a man a knight, to invoke Camelot or Excalibur, is not escapism. It is to place events within the symbolic language that cultures instinctively understand. Myth shows us the way, not as fantasy but as orientation.

For years I have studied, written, and taught these archetypes. What interests me about John Mappin is precisely this: that he reaches for myth not as decoration but as truth-telling.

He recognised in Donald Trump not just a politician but a figure cast in the oldest moulds of leadership, the knight who enters the wasteland and dares to ask the forbidden question. It is here, in that convergence of symbol and action, that the prophetic power of myth is revealed.

The Grail Quest of Sanity

In Wolfram von Eschenbach's *Parzival*, the knight fails his first test by remaining silent. He sees the king's wound but dares not ask, "What ails you?" Only later, when he learns compassion and courage, does he ask the question that heals the land.

Our age faces the same test. We can remain silent, afraid to question psychiatry, globalism, censorship, and lies. Or we can dare to ask: What ails our civilisation? Why are our borders erased? Why is truth forbidden? Trump, for Mappin, is Parzival, mocked by courts, ridiculed by elites, yet willing to ask the questions that could heal the land.

This is why Mappin links Trump to Camelot. The Restoration of Sanity is not a slogan but a Grail quest. If psychiatry is the sorcery that calls truth madness, then the Grail is truth itself, guarded by myth, waiting for knights to arise. Trump is one such knight, but the quest is larger than one man. Camelot is not nostalgia, but a reminder that the land can be healed when the forbidden questions are asked.

To read a leader, Mappin believes, you must read his mother. So he flew to Tong, near Stornoway in the Outer Hebrides while Trump was still a candidate, where Mary Anne MacLeod Trump was born. There he traced a thread running back into the Hebridean Revival. He learned of a priest, of an altar boy named Donald who grew into a minister, and a

Bible that was passed down through the revival and later gifted to Mary Anne. Decades afterward, that very Bible now sits in the Oval Office.

In that wind-carved place, Mappin found confirmation of what he had long suspected: that beneath the showmanship ran a current of faith. The laughter and the theatrics might dominate the headlines, but there was a seriousness beneath, an inheritance older than television and politics. For Mappin, the discovery did not decorate the story; it completed the pattern. Myth meets mother, symbol meets soil. And in that joining, the figure on the stage ceased to be a spectacle and became what the old tales always promised. Not a performer, but a man summoned to a vocation

It was this conviction that guided Mappin when President Trump was due to meet Queen Elizabeth II. He felt the press were determined to script the encounter as a diplomatic disaster, a clash of worlds. So he wrote to Her Majesty. In that letter he described the spiritual vein he had traced through Mary Anne MacLeod Trump and the Hebridean Revival. He reminded the Palace that both Donald and Melania were devout Christians.

Through Mappin's longstanding friendship with Charlie Kirk on the other side of the Atlantic, he ensured that President Trump knew human details such as the pet names of the Queen's corgis and reminded the president of her deep love of horses.

The Palace replied with warmth. And when the meeting came, it went better than the commentators had predicted. Against the choreography of derision, two worlds recognised one another.

Camelot, in Mappin's hands, is theatre and symbol at once: a hotel, a media hub, a fortress of myth. Those who pass through its gates sense the weight of history. They understand that the real battles are fought not with swords but with words, not with armies but with ideas and interventions.

The Living Camelot

It is noteworthy that a large, framed picture of President Donald Trump, alongside Lady Melania Trump, and together with John Mappin, hangs above the lobby in Camelot Castle. The three of them were photographed during Mappin's invitation to meet the president in 2017. A testimony to Mappin's foresight and conviction.

The honorary knighthood bestowed on Trump was an act of mythic defiance, a declaration that leadership is sacred and truth worth honouring. In a world drowning in cynicism, Mappin invoked the old language of knights and banners to remind Britain of its soul.

For him, President Trump is not saviour but warrior. One knight among many in the fight to heal the wasteland of the West. Like Parzival before the Grail, he embodies the courage to ask what others fear. The Restoration of Sanity is thus a Grail quest. A journey through deception and despair toward truth, healing, and sovereignty.

The Camelot of old is alive and well on the Cornish cliffs. Here, myth and politics meet, and knights are made not by royal decree but by courage. And as long as men like Mappin dare to honour truth, the wasteland will not have the last word.

CHAPTER FOUR

The War for the Mind

When Sanity Becomes Rebellion

How do you fight a war no one can see? Not with banners on a battlefield, but with a single decision, to keep your mind. Heroes are not forged only in combat. They are forged when a culture declares that dissent is illness, that conscience is a symptom, and that truth must be managed. The Restoration of Sanity begins there, at the moment a free man or woman refuses to surrender inner sovereignty.

Before we go further, I ask you to read with an open mind. The return to psychiatry here is intentional, not redundant. It is the hinge of John Mappin's worldview, and it is central to the claims this book explores about sovereignty, truth, and the shaping of public life.

You may not share Mappin's convictions. You may not warm to President Trump or Nigel Farage. That is beside the point. The value of inquiry is not in liking the subjects; it is in testing the ideas. Our own included.

Psychiatry, in Mappin's frame, sits at the crossroads where ideas harden into power. It conditions how we see one another, and how quickly we dismiss one another. It encourages labels in place of listening, diagnosis in place of debate, compliance in place of conscience.

If it is true that we have been taught to pathologise disagreement, then the first casualty is nuance, the second is empathy, and the third is liberty.

So what follows is not doctrine but dialogue. Read it as inquiry in the old Socratic sense: a testing of the ground beneath our feet. I have built much of my own educational ethos on this form of questioning, and it runs through my career as a writer too. The discipline is simple but difficult. Hold your convictions strongly but hold your curiosity stronger still.

The Last Frontier of Sovereignty

The story of President Trump's rise, and John Mappin's recognition of him as a knight before the world caught on, shows how myth can be a weapon of restoration. But if the vision of Camelot gives us hope, the shadows must also be named. For Mappin, the most insidious adversary is not an army on the march or a parliament in betrayal, but something quieter.

In his worldview, psychiatry is not just bad science. It is a system of control, a velvet gauntlet for the fist of power. It is the doctrine that teaches nations to doubt themselves, families to distrust each other, and individuals to see their very thoughts as symptoms. If immigration represents the physical siege and propaganda the cultural siege, then psychiatry is the psychological siege, the war for the mind.

Mappin and CCHR

This conviction is not academic for John Mappin. It is embodied in his role as an international commissioner for the Citizens Commission on Human Rights, or CCHR. To some, it is a curious footnote. To Mappin, it is aligned with a half century long crusade.

Founded in 1969, CCHR declared open war on psychiatry. Its rhetoric was unflinching, psychiatry was not just mistaken, it was destructive, a pseudo religion of coercion masquerading as care. Campaigns bore titles like Psychiatry, An Industry of Death, this lanced the boil of festering incompetence and societal harm that this so-called science had perpetrated for decades. The chaos merchants wailed but sanity was on the march. More whistleblowers came forward, supporters called it truth telling.

The commission assembled a global board of sympathetic doctors, lawyers, campaigners, and academics. Jan Eastgate would become its international president. Bruce Wiseman led its American branch. Dr. Thomas Szasz himself, one of the twentieth century's sharpest critics of psychiatry, helped to found CCHR and endued it with his philosophical credibility. Against the tide of mainstream acceptance, they raised the alarm, psychiatry does not heal, it manages, labels, controls.

Mappin's role as commissioner ties him to this lineage. From Camelot Castle he has become known as a defender of sovereignty, a supporter of Trump and Farage, a critic of globalism. CCHR fits into this pattern, the sentinel aligning with those who challenge the authorised narrative, those who refuse to accept that the state may trespass into the human soul.

Psychiatry in the Culture Wars

Mappin does not leave the critique at the level of organisational ties. His Substack writings bristle with the same energy, casting psychiatry not just as bad medicine but as a cultural weapon.

'In the culture wars of the twenty-first century,' he writes, 'few developments are as disquieting as the sight of increasing numbers of young men declaring themselves transgender. On the surface, it is presented as liberation, as discovering one's true self. But look deeper, and you see two forces working hand in glove, propaganda and psychiatry.'

It is, in his view, no grassroots revolution but cultural sabotage. He traces a pipeline. Young men told they are oppressors, internalising shame. Then directed by psychiatrists, psychologists, and clinicians into diagnosis, medication, hormones, and surgery. A generation erased under the banner of progress.

Mappin's language is blunt. 'Psychiatry is not the cure. It is the disease.' His pen does not hesitate to link today's trends with psychiatry's long record of serving ideology, lobotomies, electroshock, eugenics, Tavistock's experiments, MKUltra. For him, the pattern is clear. Psychiatry never apologises, never reforms. It adapts to the latest orthodoxy and provides the tools to enforce it.

From Camelot to Substack, from CCHR's campaigns of the nineteen seventies to the debates of today, the drumbeat is the same. Psychiatry is not neutral. It is an ally of power.

The Dark History of Psychiatry

To grasp why Mappin speaks so fiercely, one must face psychiatry's history, a history too often sanitised.

In the early twentieth century, psychiatrists across Europe and America were leading advocates of eugenics. Declaring entire populations unfit, they promoted compulsory sterilisation. Tens of thousands lost the ability to have children by decree of doctors who believed themselves scientific guardians of the race.

In Nazi Germany, psychiatry slid into atrocity. The so called T4 program systematically killed disabled mentally ill patients, the life unworthy of life. The concentration camps were foreshadowed in the wards of psychiatric hospitals, where the killing began with the authority of doctors.

After the war, psychiatry did not disappear. It evolved. In the United States, the CIA's MKUltra program enlisted psychiatrists to run experiments in brainwashing and mind control. Patients were drugged with LSD, subjected to hypnosis, sensory deprivation, and sleep deprivation. Consent was a fiction. Many never recovered.

In the nineteen fifties and sixties, lobotomies were hailed as miracle cures. They left tens of thousands brain damaged. Electroshock was administered without consent, often as punishment. Even in the modern era, the mass prescription of antidepressants and antipsychotics has created a medicated population, many trapped in cycles of dependency and withdrawal.

This is the lineage against which Mappin positions himself. Psychiatry, he argues, has consistently been more about political control than healing, reshaping individuals to fit the needs of state, institution, or ideology.

Sovereignty and the Struggle for Liberty

Here the argument sharpens into its larger frame. Mappin insists that psychiatry cannot be seen in isolation. It is a symptom of a broader disease, the erosion of sovereignty.

If psychiatry can pathologise dissent, then politics itself can be medicalised. If a child can be medicated into compliance, then an entire generation can be conditioned to obedience. If a culture can be told its traditions and masculinity are disorders, then the nation itself can be hollowed out.

This, Mappin warns, is the frontier of sovereignty. For the real question is not who governs parliaments, but who governs the mind. If governments, corporations, and global institutions can claim jurisdiction over thought, then liberty itself is dissolved.

CCHR, then, becomes not simply an anti-psychiatry group, but a frontline in the defence of freedom. Its mission is sovereignty over the soul.

Psychiatry as Geopolitical Weapon

The implications stretch beyond clinics and hospitals. Psychiatry has been woven into global governance. The World Health Organization issues guidelines that blur into mandates. United Nations conventions codify ideology in the language of rights. NGOs funded by pharmaceutical corporations lobby governments to adopt policies that reshape entire cultures.

The banner words are equity, inclusion, wellbeing. The effect is conformity. Nations that resist are shamed, sanctioned, or ostracised. Parents who question the medicalisation of their children are branded extremists. Journalists who investigate the pharmaceutical pipeline are accused of spreading misinformation. Political leaders who dissent are treated as threats to democracy.

In this light, psychiatry is not parochial but geopolitical. It becomes a tool to discipline nations, to harmonise cultures under global management. The white coat and the prescription pad become instruments of empire.

The Great Reset of the Mind

Much has been said of the World Economic Forum's Great Reset. Commentators focus on economics, digital currencies, carbon credits, central banks. But Mappin argues that the deeper reset is psychological. To control a population, one must control its mind. Psychiatry provides the architecture.

The United Nations Sustainable Development Goals wrap cultural engineering in the language of health and wellbeing. The World Health Organization's pandemic treaty claims sweeping authority over national health systems, including powers to declare emergencies and dictate responses. All justified as following science.

The danger is not only overreach, but the normalisation of overreach. Once populations accept psychiatric intrusion into their private lives, they will accept global institutions dictating the terms of their freedom.

Camelot and Resistance

Mappin's commissioner role, then, is not an obscure line on a résumé. It is a declaration of battle lines. He stands with those who resist the empire of psychiatry, who refuse to surrender sovereignty of the mind.

Camelot Castle is a symbol of that resistance. From its battlements Mappin aligns with knights of old, declaring that the mind is sacred ground. Sovereignty begins within. No parliament, no corporation, no global institution can own it.

In this sense, the war against psychiatry is not a sideshow. It is the front line of liberty. And the Restoration of Sanity is not only a metaphor. It is the Grail quest of our time. To free the soul from the machinery of control, to remind nations that their destiny is not to be managed but to be lived.

Manufactured Conflict

Drawing on the political framework Mappin employs, he explains that when former allies suddenly find themselves in conflict, it is usually because a hidden actor is whispering into one side or both, stoking grievances for their own gain.

He applies this observation to culture, to media, and to psychiatry. The quarrels that fracture families, the schisms that split movements, the panic that turns neighbours into enemies. These do not arise in a vacuum. They are often midwifed by interests that profit when trust collapses. The diagnostic label can be that hidden whisper. The sensational headline can be its echo.

In this light he calls out one of the most enduring slogans in modern mental health, the claim of a chemical imbalance in the brain. For Mappin it is advertising in a lab coat, a story crafted to sell pills rather than a measurable condition that has ever been demonstrated. A population persuaded that its disquiet is a permanent defect becomes a population available to permanent management. The result is not liberty. It is sedation presented as care.

Mappin extends the critique to the press. The message is simple, that the other fellow is dangerous. It is a script that turns politics into therapy sessions conducted by censors. In place of debate, there is diagnosis. In place of persuasion, there is shaming. In place of truth seeking, there is narrative management. He argues that this is not a flaw. It is a tactic that keeps societies anxious, divided, and therefore governable - although in the long-run renders them ungovernable.

Against this architecture of isolation, Mappin posits a rival definition of power- friendship. Real power is not the ability to coerce but the ability to help, to create bonds of mutual aid that cannot be easily infiltrated by hidden third parties. A nation that recovers the art of friendship becomes resilient. In this sense, the restoration of sanity is a social act. It is the rebuilding of fellowship at scale.

Simplicity and Spiritual Intelligence

Mappin also insists that the antidote to manipulation is often simplicity. He admires leaders who can frame complicated realities in clear terms, the equivalent of asking plainly for a cup of tea rather than accepting a complicated brew made by committee. He roots this clarity in a spiritual register, the conviction that truth is not a labyrinth but a light, and that discernment is possible when one refuses to be dazzled by jargon. This spiritual intelligence, as he presents it, is precisely what the technocratic priesthood seeks to pathologise.

The same dynamics, he argues, corrode public life. Political actors who enter with good intentions find themselves neutralised by a system that rewards conformism, tempts with gossip and vice, and collects compromising material like trophies. When such people then sign off on psychiatric regimes that medicalise dissent, they are not acting as healers of the nation, they are acting as administrators of managed decline. Sovereignty drains away not in a single betrayal, but in a thousand clinical forms.

The Battle for Liberty

Because the manipulation is psychological, Mappin counsels discipline. Resist the invitation to rage. Refuse the staged provocation. Build peaceful, professional, and persistent forms of civic action. Prevention is the cure. The less a people can be goaded, the less the white coat and the headline can justify new rounds of control.

Finally, he argues for a practice that psychiatry and media both discourage. Talking to people you think you hate. Real dialogue breaks the third party spell. It reveals common loves, common fears, and common ground. It is the opposite of pathologising an opponent. It is the decision to regard the other not as a case to be managed, but as a neighbour to be persuaded.

Whether one agrees with every claim or not, the fact is plain. Mappin has chosen his ground. He stands against the white coat when it masks authority, against the prescription pad when it replaces conscience, against the institution when it betrays truth.

The struggle for sovereignty will not be decided in parliaments alone. It will not be settled by elections or treaties. It will be decided in the hearts and minds of those who refuse to surrender. And that is why, for Mappin, the fight against psychiatry is in truth the fight for liberty itself.

If the Socratic method teaches us anything, it is that liberty survives only where questions are permitted and voices are heard. Silence them, and you do not simply lose debate. You lose civilisation itself. Psychiatry, in John Mappin's view, has become one of the engines of that silence, pathologising disagreement and teaching societies to fear their own thoughts. Its work is division: families fractured, friendships poisoned, nations taught to distrust themselves. The moment a people accept that dissent is disease, they invite tyranny through the front door.

John Mappin learned this not in abstraction but in the fate of one of his dearest and closest friends, Charlie Kirk. His story is no footnote. It is a warning written in blood. It is a testament to what happens when division is stoked, when truth is branded too dangerous to live, and when a peacemaker is struck down for daring to build unity.

And so, from the war for the mind, we turn to the life and death of a peacemaker knight.

PART THREE

THE RESTORATION OF SANITY

CHAPTER FIVE

Charlie Kirk -
The Peacemaker Knight

Themessage T he news came with the sting of unreality. John Mappin, so often the herald of bold proclamations and the prophet of hard truths, found himself instead the bearer of grief. His dearest friend, Charlie Kirk, had been assassinated in America. The shock was not confined to one family, or one nation. It was a tremor felt across the movement for sovereignty and liberty worldwide.

Mappin's words, which I received in a personal message shortly after the atrocity, were raw: 'We cannot express in words the deep sadness that my wife and I feel. It is all the more painful as we were due to see Charlie in Phoenix, Arizona this weekend, in two days' time.' In those lines lay both the personal and the political. A friendship cut short, a comrade in arms silenced, and yet a legacy instantly magnified.

Charlie Kirk was not merely a commentator or a strategist. He was, to John and Irina, a peacemaker and a dear friend. That was Mappin's first impression and his lasting testimony. He knew Charlie as one who loved his country fiercely but hated unnecessary wars. One who believed the true task of statesmanship was not to escalate division but to prevent it.

That truth was not lost on others. In September 2025, *The Telegraph* ran a major feature on the friendship between John Mappin and Charlie Kirk. The piece was written by Celia Walden, journalist, author, and wife of commentator Piers Morgan, and it captured in striking detail both the intimacy of their bond and the wider cultural impact of Kirk's mission.

Walden's article opened with Mappin's recollection of his final meeting with Kirk, a dinner at the Mandarin Oriental in Knightsbridge followed by a stroll in Hyde Park. By then, Kirk had begun to travel with security. Yet, despite the danger that increasingly surrounded him, their conversation turned not to fear but to faith and mortality.

Mappin remarked, "We discussed it, and here's the thing, he wasn't fearful. He wasn't afraid of dying at all. I've been thinking about that a lot since last Wednesday, and I am sure that's a quality people who are aware of their own eternal nature have. For Charlie, his Christian faith gave him that."

The First Encounter

Their friendship began in December 2018, when John and Irina Mappin had the singular honour of welcoming Charlie Kirk and introducing him to the United Kingdom.

What started as a modest dinner for twenty ended up being a packed VIP reception for 150 people at London's Royal Automobile Club The RAC to welcome Charlie Kirk and Candace Owens.

Many of London's cultural and social aristocracy attended. Amanda Eliasch (ex-wife of billionaire Johan Eliasch) made three phone calls and the word was out. Charlie and Candace's arrival in London was the hottest ticket that entire Christmas social season. The event was beautifully arranged. Irina and John, Peter Southall (one of London's most dynamic property developers) and Lord and Lady Tyrone Plunket headlined the evening. Mappin, joked in an aside, "By the time we had added Tyrone's cousins to the guest list we needed a bigger room."

It was billed as, 'A Gathering of Political Genius, The Introduction of a Fresh New Political Philosophy, A Solution to Cultural Marxism.'

Among the people that wanted to meet Charlie in London were, Commander in Chief of London's social orbits night club impresario Robin Birley, Ben and Zac Goldsmith, Nigel Farage of course who had noticed Charlie in America as a rising star came to say hello, the much acknowledged éminence grise of UK politics Andy Wigmore and uniquely London's Italian connection, Ciro Orsini 'The Grey Pope of London' who attended the RAC evening with his usual dramatically aesthetic entourage of eastern beauties.

Mappin recalls, "Ciro called me the very next day at 10.00. In his Italian English Ciro, a man of few words was enthused - I can't quite do his Vatican style accent."

"John, Charlie - He's good. Look after him. And Candace... she's going to be big... Take care of her, whatever you need, John, whatever you need, you let me know."

So a nod from Ciro, a Godfather to so many of Hollywood's stars and European powers, in entertainment, international business and geopolitics from Bali to Baghdad.

"Yes, but everyone there knew that what we had seen and witnessed that night was different. It was spiritual," explained Mappin.

"People sensed that they were witnessing history, and I suppose in a sense they were. So many people felt that we were part of a significant shift, it was, Candace and Charlie's speeches and the way they answered questions, had caused an eternal fracture and recomposition of the philosophical space time continuum of not just London and British Culture, but also of the world. The evening progressed to 5 Hereford

Street, Birley's private London club where a smaller dinner had been arranged by Robin. I recall it well, because Robin took us to his private dining room and introduced Charlie and Candace to General Petraeus. Charlie was absolutely honoured and delighted."

Together they launched Turning Point UK, a bold transplant of Kirk's American movement into British soil. It was more than a political event. It was a moment of cultural transfer, a recognition that the fight for sovereignty and sanity did not end at the Atlantic.

They dined together, made plans together, and forged a bond that went beyond politics. "Charlie always understood where I was coming from, and I believe I understood him," Mappin recalled. That mutual recognition, of philosophy, of faith, of mission, became the foundation of a deep and long lasting friendship.

Mappin had expressed in his introduction, the idea at that time that Charlie and Candace's visit to London was the most historically significant visit of American leaders in political philosophy to Europe since Jefferson's visit to Paris on August 6th, 1784.

In Germany, Mappin connected Charlie and Candace with H.S.H. Princess Gloria von Thurn und Taxis an old family friend, but also a prime mover in Vatican circles and a conservative grandee in international politics, "Gloria was one of the very first champions of Vice President JD Vance. Gloria spotted JD very early, before he was even a senator," Mappin explained.

Other philosophical grandees recognised Charlie, some publicly, and some privately.

Shortly after his initial visit to London, Charlie returned. On 1st February 2019 John and Irina introduced Charlie Kirk to His Grace the Duke of Marlborough at a private lunch at the Ritz.

Irina and John had felt that James and Charlie would get on. And get on they did. The Duke later commented "Charlie Kirk was a fine example of an American gentleman. He held the greatest political promise of any person of his generation."

Over that lunch, key global conflicts and issues were discussed and ways to calm them and a way forward to achieve resolution. A private text exchange that occurred after that lunch that is reprinted here with the permission of the Duke, shows just how strong the connection was.

What a privilege to meet Charlie.

What a brilliant individual.

Thank you both for a wonderful lunch and stimulating meeting with Charlie... I was so impressed...

Love to you and Irina.

Irina Mappin replied:

You were spectacular James.

You were spot on, on everything and just took our historic lunch to a whole new level.

There is no question that we shifted this world in a new direction of sanity.

Charlie was blown away by you.

Millions of people will win from your friendship with Charlie and with the President (Trump).

Irina

John later wrote these words to Charlie about their meeting; when he was already on his flight back to DC.

Dear Charlie,

Having thought through this meeting you should know that the new level of friendship forged this afternoon gives you and all those present a piece on the chessboard of life that is totally unique and very special.

I can't begin to tell you the positive impression that you created.

I am sure that His Grace was serious in ALL that he suggested.

The one thing that destructive personalities can be relied upon to do well is to work as a team - to take down and to destroy constructive people.

The primary mistake that constructive personalities make is that they tend to work on their own. This makes them vulnerable to a team of albeit much weaker individuals.

The smart thing to do is to create a team of good guys.

What happened this afternoon was that an upper level team of good guys was founded.

What games we will play in the direction of that purpose, we are totally open for life and for God to reveal.

It was one of the most important meetings we have witnessed.

John

Charlie's succinct reply captured what we all innately sensed and knew to be true.

AMEN. It was worth the entire trip.

From Blenheim Palace, the Duke later put his words into action in many ways. He warmly championed and welcomed Charlie to London where he headlined and spoke at a Gala Dinner to help with the expansion of Turning Point UK and helped bring sane discourse into being on a host of other subjects.

In one filmed interview the Duke expressed how he would chat with John, "Sometimes until the early hours until the phone battery ran out." More often they mutually arrived upon sane resolutions, ideas that brought the world closer to peace were shared with Charlie by John or by Irina with Erika.

Irina Mappin recalls how Erika Kirk, and the Duke really hit it off over dinner, "James was extremely impressed with Erika, Erika was seated next to James. Of course he has a wonderful sense of humour, so his wit precipitated a great deal of laughter, Nigel Farage and his partner Laure were seated at the same table with them and everyone just got on great."

A team of Freedom fighters and those who prefer sanity to insanity, the newly created team of good guys, had well and truly formed and was now bringing order and sanity to bear in London and in Europe. It still is ongoing.

Perhaps most importantly for Charlie and for Turning Point USA was the magnifying effect that that London evening, and subsequent meetings, had due to the connections that were created on the other side of the Atlantic in America for him by John. The initial gathering of political Genius in London had been filmed, significant supporters in the USA and new friends that Mappin introduced to Charlie were extremely impressed by Charlie's now international expansion. In the next twelve months TPUSA experienced its greatest period of expansion.

By October 31st, 2019, Charlie wrote gratefully to John and Irina and stated:

John, you and Irina have been the 2019 change maker for us.
Charlie Kirk.

Turning Point and the Global Awakening

Charlie Kirk's achievement with Turning Point USA was staggering, especially for one so young. Founded in 2012 with little more than determination and vision, TPUSA has grown into one of the most influential conservative youth organisations in America. Its mission was simple yet revolutionary: equip young people to defend the principles of free markets, limited government, and individual liberty.

At a time when universities had become temples of conformity, Turning Point created a counter culture. Campus by campus, it planted chapters that dared to speak truths considered forbidden. Students handed out literature against socialism, debated free markets in lecture halls, and proudly waved the American flag in places where it had become fashionable to sneer at patriotism.

The establishment panicked. Media outlets painted Turning Point as dangerous. University bureaucrats tried to shut down chapters. Protesters shouted down events. Yet the movement only grew. By 2020, TPUSA was present on more than two thousand campuses and had mobilised thousands of young people who no longer felt alone.

Charlie thrived in this storm. He debated opponents twice his age with ease, not with sneering cynicism but with conviction grounded in history and faith. He became a household name in America, adored by students, vilified by progressives, but impossible to ignore.

And crucially, his influence leapt the Atlantic. With John and Irina Mappin's support, Turning Point UK was launched to carry the same mission: to awaken the youth of Britain to their heritage and responsibility. TPUK held rallies, produced content, and trained young activists who would otherwise have been drowned in the tide of cultural despair.

For Mappin, this was more than an organisation. It was a living myth, proof that the youth, written off by the elites as irredeemably lost to globalist ideology, could rise again.

The Telegraph Anecdotes: Hyde Park, Windsor Castle, and the Queen

In the Telegraph article, Mappin remembered how Kirk's Christian conviction radiated through every part of his life. To those around him, it was tangible, almost otherworldly:

"It was spiritual. And he was completely committed, spiritually committed, to the idea of free speech. He also had a certainty of his own immortality that was palpable. When you were around him, you knew that you were dealing with a being that was operating on a spiritual plane. Charlie had a relationship with Christ that was unashamed and so refreshing."

The resonance of Kirk's mission even reached Windsor Castle. Shortly before the launch of Turning Point UK, John and Irina Mappin's friends, Lord and Lady Plunket, briefed Queen Elizabeth II and Prince Philip about the new organisation during tea at Windsor.

Mappin told me, "Prince Philip found it fascinating, while she just loved the idea that Charlie was bringing younger people back to the Church."

Mappin emphasised what mattered most to the late Queen:

"As a deeply Christian soul herself, she did appreciate Charlie's sincere love of Jesus Christ, and what he was doing to remind people of Christian values and to bring new people to the Church. She was very interested, encouraging and validating of what Charlie was doing."

The impact of Kirk's presence in Britain was unmistakable. Mappin recalled the RAC Club launch as a moment that struck like flint to steel.

"Charlie lit a touch paper. He did something to the British."

In the days following his death, Mappin also reflected on the mixture of grief and hostility that poured forth. While tens of thousands of young people rushed to join Turning Point chapters in Kirk's honour, there was also an unsettling wave of celebratory hatred from a minority of voices online and in British institutions. Yet Mappin held to his conviction:

"The vast majority of people in this country are completely and utterly decent. It's a very small number of people who are out-and-out evil. But I do think that the solution is to have zero-tolerance anti-violence laws, and to apply those laws."

Kirk himself had always brushed off hostility. When Mappin once warned him about British media attacks during the early days of Turning Point UK, Charlie replied in characteristic fashion:

"Not to worry. It's not going to get in our way. We just carry on."

Even after his assassination, Mappin saw the scope of Kirk's work continuing to expand:

"Everyone would say to him, 'You should be president', and he was so humble. He would always reply, 'Whatever God has in mind for me.' But he was an absolute kingmaker. Trump saw him as a son. They were so close. They would communicate and speak regularly, and Trump listened. He would sound Charlie out because he knew Charlie had his finger on the pulse, that he just knew the detail."

Mappin concluded his reflections with words that carried the weight of prophecy:

"Because we talk about turning points, and maybe it's now? Let's hope it's now, and that this is the lowest point, because in one week we've watched a young Ukrainian have her throat slit, and a person of good will get shot. So if the turning point is not now, when?"

Victories and Controversies

Turning Point did not rise quietly. It was constantly embroiled in controversy, and Charlie did not flinch from it.

When student activists were assaulted for daring to set up Turning Point stalls, Charlie used the incidents to spotlight the hypocrisy of so-called tolerant campuses. When the media tried to smear the organisation as extremist, he welcomed the attacks as evidence that the establishment was afraid. When donors were pressured to back down, he reminded them that freedom has always had a price.

Turning Point also created a media empire of its own. Through conferences like the Student Action Summit and AmericaFest, Charlie brought tens of thousands of young conservatives together under one roof, an extraordinary feat in an era when the left claimed to own youth culture.

Critics called it indoctrination. Supporters called it education. For Mappin, it was something more: the planting of Round Tables across the world, each a gathering of knights willing to defend sovereignty and truth in their own generation.

The Peacemaker's Heart

Yet beyond politics and activism, it was Charlie's faith and his profound dislike of unnecessary war that marked him most profoundly. Mappin called him a peacemaker, and it was not a casual epithet.

Charlie understood that real leadership is not measured by the wars one starts but by the wars one prevents. Behind the fiery speeches and the fearless activism, his heart was attuned to peace. He wanted a world where children inherited not endless conflict but the chance to live free.

Here Mappin's own philosophy of friendship dovetailed perfectly with Charlie's mission. In his interview shortly before Charlie's death, Mappin said: "If you have one friend you can count on, you're a wealthy person. If you've got five, you're in the super-rich." For him, power is never about armies or bank accounts but about friendship. "The fundamental of power is friendship. The fundamental of friendship is help."

That conviction was lived out in Charlie's own activism. His goal was never conquest for its own sake but the building of a community of friends, allies, and compatriots who would stand together when tested. "United we stand, divided we fall," Mappin would say, and he often said Charlie embodied that maxim in both word and deed.

Charlie's peace-making spirit was also grounded in communication. John had long argued that "there is no problem on earth with anybody that cannot be solved by communication. It takes willingness to talk to people you hate, to listen to ideas you utterly disagree with, and to find something in the other fellow to admire." For Mappin, Charlie Kirk was proof of this principle in action. A man who could stand firm without hatred, and who sought to win people over through conviction rather than coercion.

That spirit was perhaps most visible in Jerusalem. John, Irina, their son Caspian, Charlie Kirk, and Erika, who would soon become Charlie's beloved wife, walked the streets of the holy city together. Guided by Charlie, who knew Jerusalem intimately, they visited the City of David, even accessing areas not yet open to the public. There, where Christ had preached a message of love that changed history, four friends dreamed of what might yet be possible if men and women of good will gathered behind a cause of peace.

It was a pilgrimage of both faith and friendship. They prayed, they laughed, and they imagined a future where Turning Point's mission could extend beyond politics into something larger. A cultural and spiritual awakening.

A Christian Knight

Charlie Kirk's Christian faith was not an ornament but a foundation. Few, Mappin observed, had faith as strong. It gave him both courage and humility. It kept him grateful in the face of success, and unbowed in the face of hostility.

When Charlie spoke at the Oxford Union shortly before his death, Mappin was there again. They dined the evening before with old friends, the same group who had welcomed Charlie to Britain years before. Over dinner, Charlie spoke not of himself but of gratitude to God. He marvelled at how much he had already been allowed to achieve. It was the humility of a man who knew he was only a steward, never the master.

This, too, is why Mappin called him a knight. Not by title, but by spirit. For the knight's task is to stand between the people and the dragons of their age. To fight not for conquest but for peace. To wield power in defence of truth.

The Shared Vision

John Mappin and Charlie Kirk were, in many ways, cut from the same cloth. Both saw politics not as mere policy but as philosophy. Both believed sovereignty was sacred, not negotiable. Both understood that behind the noise of economics and elections lies a deeper battle; for the minds and souls of nations.

They were also mythmakers. Charlie created Turning Point not only as a political tool but as a story, a counter narrative to the despair and division sown by the establishment. Mappin, from Camelot, did the same, framing his battles in the language of knights and Round Tables. Together, they formed a transatlantic brotherhood, each reinforcing the other's conviction that truth and liberty could still prevail.

Charlie's assassination is a wound, not only to friends and family but to the movement he embodied. Yet in the mythology that frames John Mappin's life, such losses are never final. Just as Arthur's knights fall but their memory strengthens the quest, so too does Charlie's death galvanise those who remain.

"Charlie Kirk, his philosophy, and his work will never be forgotten," Mappin declares. "If anyone had the idea that such an evil act could stop his ideas, their attempt has failed utterly."

For Mappin, Charlie's death is both tragedy and a summons. A reminder that the battle is real, the costs high, but the cause righteous.

James Marlborough called John and Irina on hearing the news from Utah. It was a tough day. The Duke was sombre and poignant in his communication.

Charlie Kirk showed more political promise than any young man of his generation. He changed the world and its political philosophy forever. He was without question destined for the US Presidency. What a tragedy it is that the world will not be blessed by that. I will always remember him. I will never forget the joy with which he took up vital issues and worked to make things happen, and he did make them happen.

And that beautiful love that he had for his wife Erika.

May God Rest His Soul.

Ciro Orsini, who had not seen Charlie since that very first evening in London, sent condolences within one hour of the news of his assassination.

> *I loved him from day one when we met and thank you John for bringing Charlie Kirk into our life.*
>
> *My prayers are with you all for him and his wife Erika and his two children.*
>
> *May God bless his soul forever.*
>
> *We Love you Charlie Kirk.*
>
> *Ciro Orsini*

To meet Charlie was to love Charlie. He just had that effect on people.

Immortalised in Faith and Memory

Charlie himself believed in spiritual immortality. He knew his faith would carry him beyond the grave. Now, as Mappin says, he is with the angels. The work he began is not ended but immortalised.

In the days after the assassination, Mappin reflected again on the symbol he had recently presented on a podcast: a brass sculpture called *Friendship into Eternity.* Two figures in the circle, one pointing to the future, their bond imperfect yet unbroken. "No friendship is perfect," Mappin explained, "but real wealth lies in having even one true friend you can count on. That sculpture, once a gesture of philosophy, has now become a memorial to Charlie himself and to millions who have experienced valuable friendships in their lives."

John and Irina have pledged to care for Erika and their children, ensuring that they know who their father was, and what he achieved.

That promise is not only familial but symbolic: a vow that the next generation will not forget.

And so Charlie Kirk becomes, in this book and in Mappin's life, one of the knights of Camelot. Not by ceremony but by essence. He fought for sovereignty, spoke for peace, and held faith as his sword and shield. He was, to John and Irina Mappin, not only a comrade but a beloved friend.

Camelot Castle now carries his memory. The Round Table has one chair empty, but the circle is not broken. For every knight who falls, another rises. And the cause continues, because the cause is greater than any one man.

As Scripture says, 'Blessed are the peacemakers, for they shall be called children of God.' In that beatitude lies Charlie's legacy. He lived as a peacemaker. He died as one. And in the halls of Camelot, his name will be remembered as part of the Restoration of Sanity itself.

Hidden Miracles

Perhaps one of the greatest lessons in life is how small conversations can have world-changing effects years down the line.

One such conversation occurred on March 16th, 2019. John and Irina Mappin were staying in Jerusalem with Charlie kirk and his then girlfriend Erika, sharing several days together that blended spiritual reflection with political insight. Over supper on their first evening, John leaned into a conversation about the future of the Golan Heights, and both he and Charlie agreed that peace demanded moral clarity and that Israel's sovereignty over the region should be recognised openly and without hesitation.

Over the following two days, as the group walked together through the old town of Jerusalem, Hebron and the City of David placing their feet in the very footsteps of Christ, visiting the exact spot where Christ exercised his freedom of speech and sovereignty, their conversation deepened.

What had begun over supper as a moment of reflection and brainstorming for a solution to an impasse that was blocking the Abraham accords from proceeding, turned into an ongoing exchange about history, prophecy, and the fragile architecture of peace. Each discussion seemed to build on the last, and by the time they stood among the ancient stones of Hebron, the idea had taken on a life of its own.

Acting on their shared inspiration, when Charlie flew by helicopter to the Golan Heights on the 18th of March with an IDF officer, from the mountain ridge, looking out across the contested landscape, Charlie called Jared Kushner to share what John and Charlie had been discussing in Jerusalem. On hearing the idea, within moments, Kushner put him directly through to President Trump walking the phone through to the Oval office which was next door to his own.

Later, at dinner that night, Charlie told John and Irina that he had spoken with President Trump personally and had shared the essence of their Jerusalem discussions. He had conveyed that recognising Israel's sovereignty over the Golan Heights would not only affirm a moral truth but would also serve as a stabilising act of leadership in a volatile region. According to Charlie, the President listened carefully, responded with warmth and decisiveness, and said he would look into the matter immediately.

Three days later, on Purim, the day in Jewish scripture, which is associated with divine will and hidden miracles, Trump tweeted: 'After 52 years it is time for the United States to fully recognise Israel's Sovereignty over the Golan Heights.' He formally signed the proclamation at the White House on 25 March beside Prime Minister Netanyahu and later declared, "Every President said they'd do it, but I did it." The move was completely unanticipated, not least in Israel where instantaneous celebrations broke out. To this day there exists a town in the Golan named Trump town to mark that decision..

Fast forward six and a half years later, and as I write this book now, on 14 October 2025, it is Charlie Kirk's Birthday and the day he was awarded the posthumous Presidential Medal of Freedom in the Rose Garden at the Whitehouse.

It is the very day after President Trump declared and signed his historic Peace Deal in the Middle East. A feat and extraordinary achievement that all but President Trump, and perhaps those present walking in the footsteps of Christ in Jerusalem on March 16-17-18 and 19th March 2019 thought was attainable.

Beverley Turner interviewed John Mappin live on GB News from Washington, D.C., on the 14th of October 2025. She gave him over eleven minutes to recount the full story.

Linking the recent Middle East peace breakthrough following the Gaza ceasefire to that original Jerusalem conversation and the Abraham Accords, Beverley highlighted how Charlie's phone call with President Trump on that day from the Golan played a role in the ceasefire years later.

John reflected on those few days staying with Charlie and Erika in Israel, walking, dining, and speaking openly of faith and leadership, and how those conversations became the spark for a chain of events far larger than any of them could have foreseen. It was proof that when conviction and divine timing meet, history itself moves.

Looking back now, it is clear why the sovereignty of the Golan Heights mattered so deeply. Without sovereignty of the Golan there could be no peace. The region was more than contested land; it was the high ground from which Israel had once been attacked and which, if left uncertain, would always threaten the fragile balance of the Middle East. To recognise it as sovereign was to replace ambiguity with truth. And peace, as John often said, cannot exist where truth is denied.

At the point of writing this book, events have unfolded and occurred in real time. Not a single week has passed without the national or international press, or a politician of high rank, mentioning John Mappin or using him as an example within the context of unfolding world events, no more so than within the context of the life and death of Charlie Kirk.

As the world turns once more toward the question of peace, we are reminded that it is not born of treaties or power alone, but of truth spoken in courage and faith shared in friendship. From small conversations come great reckonings, and in the quiet courage of those who believe, the future still waits to be written.

And therein, within the magic of such quiet and private communications, begins the inception of hidden miracles.

Toward the Next Battle

Yet the story cannot end here, because Charlie's passing is not only a wound but a summons. His work reminds us that the fight for truth and sovereignty is not fought only on the battlefield of politics, but also in the quiet yet devastating struggles over the human mind.

If Kirk was the knight who sought peace in the world of nations, John Mappin insists that the same vigilance must now be turned inward. Toward the realm of thought itself. For the greatest danger of our age may not come from armies or parliaments, but from philosophies that corrupt the very meaning of sanity and unity.

And so we turn from the story of one fallen knight to the wider war he fought alongside John Mappin: the struggle against insanity as an instrument of control, and the collapse of unity in a civilisation that has forgotten its soul.

CHAPTER SIX

The Great Unravelling of Sanity

A Call for Unity in Fractured Times

Charlie Kirk's death left a hollow space in the circle of Mappin's allies, but it did not end the mission. For Mappin, the loss of a dear friend was also the reminder of a deeper truth: unity is not optional, it is essential. The adversaries of liberty, whether they come cloaked in political power or medical authority, thrive on division. To honour Kirk is to carry forward the fight to restore cohesion in a fractured age.

At Camelot Castle, the watchword has long been simple. United we stand, divided we fall. The phrase is no slogan. It is the very heartbeat of Mappin's philosophy. Sovereignty cannot be defended by isolated individuals but only by people bound together in courage and conviction. From Cornwall's cliffs, he has sought to turn this maxim into lived reality.

Mappin has carried this belief into every sphere of his work. He has invited figures across the political spectrum to speak, dine, and debate under his roof. He has not been afraid to bring ideological opponents into the same room, convinced that dialogue, even heated dialogue, is a weapon against tyranny. Camelot is not a bubble; it is a crossroads.

One of the most human testaments to this unifying instinct came in

2019. During the launch of Turning Point UK in London, walking up the grand staircase to the Napoleon room at the RAC club, Candace Owens playfully confided in Mappin. With a laugh, Candace said that she had the idea she "Might marry an Englishman someday." Mappin, not considering himself much of a matchmaker, by way of repartee promised he would keep an eye out. Less than ten minutes later in what the Mappin's and the Farmer's now consider an extraordinary act of providence, The Honourable George Farmer, son of Lord Farmer, walked into the room. "Candace, let me introduce you to George Farmer," Mappin said.

"And the rest," as Candace and Charlie love to say, "was future!"

Eighteen days later, Candace and George were engaged. Today they are married with four beautiful children and remain close friends of the Mappins. That encounter was more than romance; it was the weaving together of two threads of cultural resistance, a bond between British conservatism and American populism forged in real human terms.

For Mappin, such stories and real life events are proof that unity and divine providence is not theoretical. It is lived, embodied, and lasting.

When Psychiatry Divides, Not Unites

Yet if unity is the foundation of sovereignty, then psychiatry, in Mappin's view, has been its great saboteur. Modern psychiatry, he insists, is not primarily a field of healing but an ideological system that pathologises dissent, emotions, and spiritual unrest. To label discomfort as clinical is to exile it from community and, in turn, to unravel the bonds that hold people together.

This is why voices like Tucker Carlson's and Dr Josef Witt-Doerring's matter. Psychiatry, long defended as hard science, is being revealed as narrative. What has been marketed as healing is, in fact, conditioning. What has been framed as compassion is, in truth, control.

Mappin had been saying this for years. Psychiatry, in his telling, does not unite communities in compassion; it fragments them in suspicion and fear. It convinces people they are broken machines, isolates them in diagnostic categories, and medicates them into silence. In place of unity, it breeds dependence. In place of resilience, it manufactures fragility.

At its most destructive, this ideology provokes and inspires physical violence.

Philosophy and the Myth of Mental Illness

Mappin's critique is not without precedent. The Hungarian-American psychiatrist Thomas Szasz, in *The Myth of Mental Illness* (1961), argued that psychiatric diagnoses are not scientific discoveries but social judgments. Mental illness, Szasz said, is a metaphor, a label society uses when it cannot tolerate difference. To call a man 'schizophrenic' or 'depressed' is less about his biology than about the community's refusal to bear his pain.

Michel Foucault, in *Madness and Civilization*, reached a similar conclusion. The asylum, he argued, was not a hospital but a prison of ideas, a mechanism by which the so-called 'Age of Reason' excluded those who did not conform. Psychiatry was never neutral science; it was discipline disguised as therapy.

Mappin has taken these critiques and driven them into the present. What Szasz saw in the 1960s and Foucault dissected in archives, Mappin sees alive today in clinics, schools, and media narratives. Psychiatry has always been about power. It is a political weapon of control. The only difference is the tools: where once it used chains and asylums, now it uses prescriptions and diagnostic manuals.

Contrast this with older traditions. The Greeks saw tragedy as a communal process of confronting suffering. Medieval Christians saw melancholy as a spiritual trial that could deepen wisdom. Romantic poets treated despair as a forge for creativity. In all these traditions, suffering was meaningful, not pathological. Psychiatry, in Mappin's eyes, has robbed us of this meaning and replaced it with sterile labels and chemical sedation.

To call this progress is, he insists, the greatest illusion of all.

Psychiatry's Role in the Epidemic of Violence

For Mappin, the failures of psychiatry are not abstract, they are written in blood. He points to America's school shootings as case studies in the dangers of psychiatric dependence.

Eric Harris, one of the Columbine killers, was prescribed Luvox. Kip Kinkel, who killed his parents before opening fire on his classmates in Oregon, had been given Prozac and Ritalin. Andreas Lubitz, the Germanwings co-pilot who deliberately crashed his plane into the Alps, killing 150, was reportedly suffering from severe psychiatric drug side effects.

"These are not anomalies," Mappin insists. "They are a pattern. The media obsesses over guns, video games, or political rage, but it refuses to touch the psychiatric connection. Silence has become complicity."

If even a small fraction of those on SSRIs experience violent ideation, the sheer scale of prescriptions makes tragedy inevitable. Tens of millions are medicated. The law of numbers ensures disaster. Yet the press, politicians, and pharmaceutical giants close ranks.

Tucker Carlson has praised Tennessee's new law requiring toxicology screens of mass shooters to test for psychiatric drugs. For the first time, a state has cracked the silence. To Mappin, it is a fissure in the wall of denial, proof that truth, however long suppressed, cannot be buried forever.

MKUltra's Ghost in Modern Psychiatry

To understand psychiatry's role today, Mappin insists, one must remember its roots. In the 1950s and 60s, the CIA's MKUltra program experimented with LSD, hypnosis, sleep deprivation, and electroshock in the quest for mind control. Patients were not healed; they were broken, studied, discarded.

Though the program was officially ended, its logic seeped into psychiatry itself. What was once crude, lobotomies and shocks, became refined into pharmaceuticals and diagnostic categories. The form changed, but the function remained: control. Every unproven diagnosis, every prescription without accountability, every label that reduces a soul to a disorder, all are echoes of MKUltra's ghost.

Mappin warns that until we confront this lineage, we will continue to misname suppressive control as care.

Unity Requires Truth and Transparency

Mappin also sees psychiatry's role in the rise of gender ideology. Where once depression was over-diagnosed, now identity confusion is pathologised. Children are funnelled into hormones and surgeries with the same institutional logic that once pushed Prozac.

What is sold as liberation is, in his view, another form of control. Families are torn apart, childhoods disrupted, communities divided.

Psychiatry provides the clinical machinery; ideology supplies the narrative. Together, they medicalise confusion and fracture unity.

Against this backdrop, Mappin calls for action:

- A public inquiry into psychiatric drug use and violence, free from government and pharmaceutical influence.

- Full transparency on prescriptions, empowering citizens with knowledge.

- Platforms where truth can be spoken without censorship, where figures like Tucker Carlson and Candace Owens can converge to challenge psychiatric orthodoxy and can open up communications that flush out the insanity that has infiltrated the life of our world to heal cultural rifts.

Camelot, in this vision, is not nostalgia. It is a Round Table for the modern age, where labels drop, conversations rise, and alliances form.

Beyond the Wasteland: The Restoration of Sanity

Yet Mappin has never wanted his campaign to become only a catalogue of horrors. His vision is twofold: to expose the lies and to illuminate the alternatives. To criticise without offering hope would be nihilism, and Camelot is anything but nihilistic. It is a living affirmation that community, creativity, faith, and sovereignty can restore sanity.

Empires collapse under abstraction, but families, towns, and friendships endure. Mappin insists that the antidote to alienation is not another pill but presence. A conversation in a great hall carries more healing than a thousand sterile consultations. Camelot is a prototype: a place where strangers become allies and suffering becomes part of the human condition, not a disorder.

The down to earth qualities and friendliness of Camelot Castle's staff themselves are testimony to this. These are decent people with their own challenges and struggles in life but endued with a higher purpose. They create a beautiful and creatively inspiring environment and atmosphere. They have become stellar names to those who have visited Camelot but at their hearts they are just ordinary folk who care about the future.

Mappin would argue that art is medicine. Music, painting, poetry. These transform pain into meaning. Modern psychiatry silences suffering; art redeems it. To create is to resist despair, Mappin says, and to resist despair is to reclaim freedom.

The crisis of the West is spiritual, not chemical. Mystics once saw despair as a dark night of the soul. Philosophers wrestled with anguish as the price of wisdom. Poets found beauty in grief. To treat suffering as pathology is to strip it of meaning. Faith, ritual, and philosophy restore what pills cannot. Purpose.

Above all, Mappin insists that the restoration of sanity begins with reclaiming sovereignty. "You are not a broken machine," he says. "You are a sovereign soul." To accept the label of patient is to surrender power. To embrace sovereignty is to awaken resilience.

It is here that myth becomes more than story. In the archetype of the hero, as Joseph Campbell and others have shown, we see the structure of human renewal. The hero begins in the ordinary world, untouched by great struggle. He is called to the quest, and at first he resists. The unknown appears more dangerous than the comforts of the familiar. Yet in time he realises that refusal is itself peril, that if he does not leave the village, the dangers will one day arrive at his door.

Only by stepping into adversity does he discover the resources hidden within, the gifts that hardship alone can awaken. At the end of the quest, the hero returns home transformed, bearing wisdom and strength that would have remained dormant had he never ventured out. This is the cycle through which cultures have always understood trial, courage, and renewal.

It is little wonder, then, that contemporary society and strands of modern psychology often reframe the mythological hero as a danger, branding him with the language of 'toxic masculinity.' This is not mere critique, but a cultural inversion. An empowering and necessary archetype recast as pathology. To strip the hero of his dignity is to deprive society of its most vital imaginative resource, the figure who teaches us that struggle is formative and courage indispensable. Far from being a threat to civilisation, the heroic archetype is one of its foundations. Properly understood, it is not a relic of an oppressive past, but a positive and enduring model for renewal in an age that has forgotten how to face trial without retreating into sedation.

As I have written many times before, most recently in *Cancel THIS*, this inversion is not a mistake. It is by design. And it is designed to disempower. It is part of the long march toward the indoctrination of the West with helpless archetypes, because a disempowered population is far easier to control. Strip away the hero, and you strip away resistance itself.

From Fragility to Strength

It is here that Candace Owens's voice joins Mappin's. Owens has warned against the mass drugging of children and the culture of fragility psychiatry has normalised. But she also offers something more: a philosophy of resilience. "If you hold a permanent view of yourself as a victim, you become your own oppressor," she declares, cutting to the heart of a cultural disease that psychiatry too often enables.

Hardship, Owens reminds us, is not a disease but a teacher. Challenges forge clarity, strength, and faith. To wallow in victimhood is to surrender agency, but to endure trials is to grow into fortitude.

Her outlook dovetails with Mappin's Restoration of Sanity. Both insist the West does not need more diagnoses or more pills. It needs courage. It needs conviction. It needs the mental strength to face hardship and emerge stronger.

Mappin, then, becomes the nexus where these voices converge. Mappin, Owens, Carlson, and others such as Rabbi Lord Jonathan Sacks, call for a culture that abandons fragility and reclaims fortitude, which refuses sedation and embraces sovereignty.

Rabbi Sacks, a great inspiration to John and Irina Mappin, and to those who value sovereignty, argued in The Dignity of Difference (2002) that God creates diversity so humanity can learn mutual respect.

United we stand. Divided we fall. And through truth, strength, and unity, the wasteland of despair can once again bloom.

CHAPTER SEVEN

The English Birthright:
A Tradition of Limits

This Far, and No Further:
The English Birthright of Liberty

The English story is, at its heart, a story of limits - limits on power, limits on tyranny, limits on those who would govern without consent. It is a tradition written not just in laws, but in blood and defiance.

It begins at Runnymede in 1215, when a reluctant King John, hemmed in by rebellious barons, sealed a parchment that would outlive him and his dynasty. Magna Carta was not democracy as we know it today, but it was the first great public stake driven into the ground. The law would stand above the ruler. No free man could be imprisoned or dispossessed without due process. Taxes could not be levied without common consent. The sovereign was not absolute.

From that moment, English liberty became something different to the continental kind. It was not granted by the state, it was wrestled from it, defended as an inheritance, and held with suspicion toward all who would expand their own authority.

Centuries later, in 1644, another voice rose to guard that inheritance, not from kings, but from Parliament itself. John Milton's *Areopagitica* was a thunderclap in an age of pamphlets and purges. Standing in the Commons, he begged them not to shackle the press under 'licensing,' arguing that the liberty to speak and write freely was not a luxury, but the lifeblood of a free people. "Give me the liberty to know, to utter, and to argue freely according to conscience," Milton declared, "above all liberties." It was an argument that still scorches across the centuries.

The same flame burned in 1689, when the Glorious Revolution produced the English Bill of Rights, securing parliamentary supremacy, free elections, and the right to petition without fear of punishment. And it would blaze again in the speeches of Edmund Burke, who saw liberty as the balance between ordered tradition and the restless urge for change, warning against the destruction of either.

Even in the twentieth century, when the threat came from abroad, the call was the same. Churchill, addressing the Commons in the dark summer of 1940, was not speaking only of tanks and air raids when he promised to "fight on the beaches." He was defending a way of life in which the individual, not the state, was the master.

This is the inheritance. Magna Carta's restraint on power, Milton's defence of truth-telling, Burke's balance, Churchill's grit. It is a chain of custody stretching across eight centuries, each link forged by those who refused to submit to arbitrary rule, whether cloaked in royal ermine or bureaucratic jargon.

And yet today, that chain is under siege, not by foreign invasion, but by an establishment that treats these rights as negotiable, conditional, even outdated. Our rulers manage speech as if it were a public health hazard, outsource sovereignty to unelected bodies, and treat the law as a tool for political convenience.

It is into this breach that John Mappin steps, not as a king, not as a party leader, but as a citizen who refuses to forget what the English are meant to be.

On the cliffs of Cornwall, with Camelot Castle flying its banner, a Dark Blue Excalibur in contrast against a white flag of peace - drawn and saluting the heavens - a bright yellow sun of hope at its hilt, flying into the brisk Atlantic wind, Mappin holds the line in his own way. His battles are modern. Immigration, censorship, institutional cowardice. But his principles are ancient. He speaks of justice, borders, and speech in the same breath as those who once argued for due process, sovereignty, the abolition of slavery, and the liberty to utter truth without fear. And he told me with typical bluntness that much of the political class today is, "Dealing in absolute stupidity that is off the charts." It is not ignorance alone that alarms him, but the wilful rejection of wisdom that England once held sacred.

In an age that prefers slogans to substance, Mappin is formidable for a simple reason: he remembers. He remembers that the English birthright was never a gift. It was a fight. And it still is.

Law, Sovereignty, and Liberty with Backbone

Mappin's worldview is forged from the steel of British history and sharpened by the crises of our age. His convictions are not the shallow, market tested 'values' of party politics, but the deeper laws of a sovereign people: law that is just, borders that are defended, and speech that is free.

It is a creed that would be instantly recognisable to Britain's great defenders of liberty, from the barons who forced King John's hand at Runnymede, to John Milton defying the censors of Cromwell's Parliament, William Wilberforce's passion to abolish slavery, to the great parliamentary rebels who resisted crown and mob alike in the name of principle.

For Mappin, this is not academic nostalgia. This is a living inheritance.

Justice Must Mean Justice

Magna Carta's first legacy was to bind power to law, to declare that no ruler, crown or council, could act without restraint. It was the beginning of the English insistence that justice must be impartial and accessible, not an indulgence granted by the powerful.

Mappin believes the modern British state has betrayed that principle, not through overt tyranny, but through neglect and cowardice. Justice today too often bends toward the criminal, not the victim. Violent offenders are released early, grooming gangs evade full accountability, knife crime ravages communities while politicians debate 'root causes' in air conditioned conference rooms.

He sees this as a violation of the Magna Carta spirit, a retreat from the ancient duty to protect the realm and the innocent. In his mind, justice must be swift, visible, and uncompromising, because the moment the public loses faith in its impartiality, they lose faith in the nation itself.

Borders Are Not Racist, They Are Necessary

The barons of 1215 did not petition King John for borderless governance. They fought for a sovereign England, one whose land, laws, and loyalties were not up for auction. Likewise, Mappin views borders not as a modern invention, but as the physical expression of sovereignty itself.

In this, he stands in a long line of English constitutionalists who saw defence of the realm as both moral duty and political necessity. The very notion of Parliament's legitimacy rests on the consent of the governed, something impossible if the government cannot, or will not, decide who belongs to the political community.

For Mappin, lax immigration enforcement, asylum fraud, and the political class's deference to foreign courts are a dereliction of that duty. A sovereign people has the right to decide who enters, who stays, and who is removed. Anything less is not compassion, it is abdication.

Speech Is Sacred

If Magna Carta chained the state's hand, Milton's *Areopagitica* sharpened the people's tongue. In 1644, Milton stood in Parliament and argued against prior censorship with words that still burn.

Mappin would sign that speech in his own blood. He is a fierce opponent of Britain's creeping censorship, whether in the form of hate speech prosecutions, pandemic era gag orders, or the new priesthood of misinformation regulators.

Like Milton, he understands that the right to speak freely is the first defence against tyranny and the last refuge of the individual. The minute speech becomes a licensed privilege instead of an inalienable right, sovereignty collapses into managed opinion, and truth becomes whatever the powerful permit.

As he once put it to me, much of the media's message boils down to a single poisonous idea, 'the other fellow over there, he's bad, he's dangerous.' It is this endless stoking of division that corrodes the possibility of a sane public square.

Tradition Meets Bold Disruption

Though rooted in tradition, Mappin does not romanticise the past. His is not the rose tinted nostalgia of the heritage brochure, but the disruptive energy of a reformer who knows that institutions either serve their founding purpose or deserve to be rebuilt.

In this he echoes the great Whig and Tory reformers alike, men who understood that the health of the constitution depended on pruning corruption, clearing bureaucratic deadwood, and confronting institutional capture.

Mappin's targets are clear; a civil service that wields power without accountability, a policing culture paralysed by paperwork and politics, a legal system so clogged with process that justice is delayed into irrelevance. He would strip them back to function, not form.

Milton fought for liberty against the overreach of both crown and Puritan Parliament. Likewise, Mappin rejects the false choice between violent extremes, whether religious theocracy or radical leftist mob rule. He sees both as forms of the same disease, the will to dominate by silencing, intimidating, or destroying dissent.

A free society must guard against sedition from without and subversion from within, not by sacrificing liberty, but by using it as a shield and sword against those who would abolish it.

Mappin's stance is not that of the career politician, bending with the wind of opinion polls. His is the posture of the independent freeholder, the self-governing citizen, the watchman on the battlements: an archetype stretching back to the fyrdmen of Alfred's England and the longbowmen of Agincourt.

His values, courage, honour, liberty, truth, are the same ones invoked by Churchill when he warned against appeasement, by Thatcher when she stood against Argentine intimidation, and by countless unknown Britons who refused to bow to foreign yokes or domestic despotism.

And like those forebears, he insists that patriotism is not a matter of convenience. It is, he told me, an, "Eternal purpose." True patriots, he argued, must be willing, "To put their duty above their personal discomfort."

Submission or Sovereignty

For Mappin, the political spectrum is a distraction. The real divide is between submission and sovereignty, between a managed decline administered by unaccountable elites and a national renaissance built on self-governance. He is fully aware that the tradition he defends is under siege not just from hostile foreign ideologies, but from Britain's own establishment, a class that treats sovereignty as an embarrassing relic. Liberty as a negotiable commodity, and truth as a liability.

Against that backdrop, Mappin's ideological compass points to the same true north it would have for Milton, for the barons at Runnymede, and for every free born Briton who refused to be a subject without consent. A people must be free to govern themselves, to guard their borders, to speak their minds, and to live under laws they respect because they had a hand in shaping them. This is not simply 'Mappin's vision.' It is the old English birthright, renewed for a nation at risk of forgetting it.

And if history teaches anything, from the parchment at Runnymede to the printed pages of *Areopagitica*, it is that such rights are never preserved by the timid. They are preserved by those willing to stand and say: this far, and no further.

The Sanity of the English Tradition

What Mappin insists upon, again and again, is that England's birthright is not just a legal inheritance but a spiritual one. A sane society, he argues, is one that remembers its rulers' limits. Kings had limits. Parliaments had limits. Even the state itself had limits. And within those limits, liberty flourished. But recognising this, and by knowing the limits of institutions and rulers, the human spirit can ethically thrive without limits.

When those limits are forgotten, madness follows. The French Revolution devoured its children because it had no ballast of tradition. The Bolsheviks drowned Russia in blood because they mistook ideology for truth and were grounded in an insane philosophy. England, by contrast, balanced change with continuity, reform with reverence. That balance is the true Restoration of Sanity, and it is what Mappin calls us back to.

Locke wrote of the social contract, Burke of the moral imagination, Milton of the liberty to utter truth without fear. These were not just political principles but safeguards of the collective mind. A people who can speak freely, govern themselves, and uphold law above rulers are a people capable of sanity.

Today, Mappin sees the same battle being fought under new banners. Bureaucrats who police misinformation are the same in spirit as censors who demanded licenses for pamphlets. Judges who bend law to ideology are the heirs of monarchs who bent justice to whim. Politicians who surrender borders to unelected courts betray the same spirit that King John displayed before the barons: power unrestrained.

And he warned me that propaganda today has become nothing less than, "Military-grade psyops, a weapon of mass destruction." It is a form of warfare not aimed at fortifications but at sanity itself.

In writing this, I am not dealing only in abstractions. During the pandemic years, I was the only headmaster or school principal, out of 43,500 in the United Kingdom, to publicly question the mass vaccination of children against Covid-19. For exercising that duty of care, I discovered that I was being monitored by the authorities. Emails and reports circulated, my words were flagged, and my integrity was quietly scrutinised. What should have been a matter of open debate was treated instead as suspicion, even subversion. It was a brush with the modern 'thought police,' the very psyops machine that Mappin warns against: a state that polices conscience under the guise of protecting health.

Such treatment is not only profoundly undemocratic. It is profoundly un-British. The very traditions of liberty and open argument that stretch from Runnymede to Milton's *Areopagitica* are violated when dissent is pathologised.

Yet equally un-British is the temptation to stay silent, to retreat, and to hope that someone else will bear the burden. Liberty has never been preserved by passivity. It has always required men and women to stand up, to fight back, and to say without apology, "this far, and no further."

This is why Mappin's call resonates so deeply. My own experience taught me that liberty is not lost in a single moment of tyranny, but in the slow corrosion of confidence, when individuals fear to speak and institutions punish those who do. To resist that corrosion is not only an act of defence. It is an act of creation. It is the choice to believe that truth is not a threat but a foundation, and that courage, even when lonely, can become contagious.

And yet Mappin's vision is not merely defensive. It is creative, reforming, hopeful. Just as Magna Carta was not the end but the beginning of English liberty, so too the Restoration of Sanity is the beginning of a new phase of sovereignty. It means rebuilding justice so that victims, not criminals, are protected. It means restoring borders so that compassion is ordered, not chaotic. It means freeing speech so that the nation can argue its way back to health.

At Camelot Castle, this vision becomes tangible. Guests from across the political spectrum gather at one table. Conversations take place without fear of censorship. Debates are vigorous but never silenced. It is not fantasy; it is practice. The Round Table is not a relic but a method: power shared, truth spoken, sanity restored.

And there is optimism here. For Mappin does not see England as finished. He sees her as wounded but not slain, like the Fisher King in Arthurian legend. What heals the Fisher King? Not force, not ideology, but a single honest question: *What ails you?* That, Mappin believes, is the question England must ask itself.

What ails our justice system? What ails our borders? What ails our speech? What ails our sovereignty? If we dare to ask, we can dare to heal.

The English birthright, then, is not nostalgia but prophecy. It is the reminder that sanity can be restored, because it has been before. Runnymede was a restoration. The Bill of Rights was a restoration. Even Churchill's defiance was a restoration of the English refusal to submit. Each generation takes up the chain, reforges the links, and hands it on.

Now it is our turn. And Mappin, standing on the Cornish cliffs, calls us to remember. Not as academics, not as spectators, but as heirs. The Restoration of Sanity is nothing less than the renewal of the English spirit: liberty bound by law, sovereignty defended with courage, and speech spoken without fear.

This is the English birthright. It is not dead. It is waiting to be claimed.

CHAPTER EIGHT

The Literary Soul of Britain - An Act of Resistance

Voices That Refuse to Bow

John Mappin has built connections with some of the most influential political leaders and media voices in the world. From his base at Camelot Castle in Cornwall, he has cultivated friendships and dialogues with presidents, prime ministers, broadcasters, and cultural figures. Yet Mappin is more than a networker or host. He is a mythmaker who sees Britain not only as a nation but as a narrative: a story shaped as much by literature and oratory as by law and policy. To understand him, one must look not only to his business ventures or political connections, but to his conviction that Britain's destiny is written in words: the words of poets, prophets, and patriots, which he now seeks to revive for a nation at risk of forgetting its soul.

Mappin is not bound by politics, defined by business, or confined to the mould of a country gentleman. He is something rarer, and more compelling. A man who owns Camelot and treats it not as real estate but as prophecy. A man who battles censorship with pageantry, media with myth, and modern decay with ancient poetry.

To understand him, forget policy papers and party manifestos. You will not find him in the House of Commons; you will find him between the lines of *Paradise Lost, Jerusalem,* and *Idylls of the King.* Mappin is less a political actor than a literary one. He is a mythmaker in a nation that has forgotten its own story.

British literature has never merely entertained. It has conjured kings, justified rebellion, and defined what it means to be a free people on sacred soil. The literary soul of Britain, what Blake called 'Albion,' is not some nostalgic relic. It is a living, aching idea. And Mappin, however unconventional his detractors may say he is, dares to keep it alive.

Mappin as Writer

To see Mappin only as a media figure is to miss his essence. He is, at heart, a writer. His Substack is not a hobby but a platform, a continuation of England's pamphleteering tradition. In the seventeenth century, Milton's pamphlets thundered against censorship. In the eighteenth, Thomas Paine's *Common Sense* stoked revolution across the Atlantic. Today, Mappin's digital essays do something similar: they ignite debates, defy orthodoxy, and appeal to conscience rather than to consensus.

He writes with urgency, sometimes blunt, sometimes poetic, often prophetic. In this he resembles the literary dissidents of old. Men who knew that words were not ornaments but weapons. For Mappin, a Substack post is not just commentary, it is battle. Each essay is a skirmish in the wider war for Albion's soul. Critics call him unconventional, but then, they said the same of Blake. They sneered at Chesterton. They censored Milton. In England, the writers who matter have always been original, unlicensed, inconvenient. Mappin is no different.

On Substack, Mappin does not write like a detached analyst but as a man addressing friends and compatriots directly. One post begins: 'The quest for sanity is one that I know that many of you my friends and followers agree is a noble undertaking.' That voice is personal, urgent and conversational. It reveals why his essays feel closer to Milton's pamphlets than to today's sterile op-eds. He is not writing at people but with them. Summoning them into dialogue.

In many ways, he belongs to the Miltonic tradition of 'unlicensed printing.' Milton argued that truth, left free to contend with falsehood, would always prevail. Mappin writes in that same defiant key. He trusts his audience to discern. He refuses to flatter them with half-truths. He writes not to soothe, but to awaken.

Mappin as Orator

But Mappin is not only a writer. He is an orator, one of the last of a dying breed in an age of managed PR and scripted soundbites. He appears on alternative channels, his voice ringing through podcasts and livestreams. He has sparred with mainstream interviewers on Fox News, and more recently on the BBC, speaking plainly where others hedge.

When John Mappin speaks, it is with a conviction that echoes England's great rhetorical tradition. Shakespeare gave us Henry V, rallying his soldiers at Agincourt with the immortal words: "We few, we happy few, we band of brothers." Those lines endure because they touch something older than politics, something woven into the English spirit. Churchill, in 1940, captured that same essence when he promised to fight on the beaches, in the fields, in the streets, until victory was secured.

Mappin does not compare himself to Churchill, but he understands the principle. Words, when spoken with sincerity, can rouse a people from despair. He refuses the sterile jargon of modern politics. His oratory is clear, moral, often moralistic, always direct. He has the courage to say what others whisper, and in saying it aloud, he breaks spells.

When he told me plainly that much of the political class is, "Dealing in absolute stupidity that is off the charts," he shrugged when he said it, as if it were not a provocation but a diagnosis. Moral clarity begins with linguistic clarity.

Even in the cynical chambers of the BBC, he speaks with the same conviction he carries on alternative channels. To him, there is no mainstream and alternative, there is only truth, and the courage to utter it. This is why he is invited back, even by those who disagree with him. His opponents recognise that he speaks with force and clarity, that he is animated by something more than vanity or party loyalty. He is animated by Albion itself.

The Word as Sword

This is why Mappin fights censorship so fiercely. He knows what every poet and prophet has known, that words make worlds. In the beginning was the Word, says St. John's Gospel. The King James Bible made this truth part of England's bloodstream. The Book of Common Prayer, recited for centuries in village churches, gave rhythm to English life. Shakespeare gave it drama. Milton gave it defiance.

To silence words, then, is to maim the soul of a people. To license speech is to dethrone liberty. Mappin's battles with censorship are not unthought through outbursts, they are a defence of the Logos itself, the ancient recognition that truth must be spoken or else the world collapses into madness.

He warned me that what now passes for messaging is often military grade psyops. A weapon of mass destruction. Not aimed at buildings, but at minds. Not at bridges, but at sanity itself. The point, he explained, is to separate a people from their story. The cure is the return of living speech.

The Literary Ethic of Friendship

Mappin's literary imagination does not float in the abstract. It incarnates in friendship. He believes that the fundamental of power is friendship, and the fundamental of friendship is help. It is a philosophy that reads like a proverb. It is also a strategy. Language binds. Friendship holds. A nation that relearns the ethic of friendship will find its voice again.

At Camelot Castle he displays a large sculpture he calls *Friendship into Eternity*. Two figures stand inside a circle. One points forward. The other steadies the ring. The piece sits like a parable on a mantel at Camelot. Literature talks about virtue. Art gives it shape.

Mappin also trusts the English character more than he trusts English institutions. "We are an eleventh hour nation, and we tend to rally at about a quarter to twelve." The line carries the rhythm of a proverb. It is not fatalism. It is hope. England may tack toward the rocks. England may flirt with amnesia. Yet England remembers in time. That memory, in his mind, begins with words and ideas.

British Literature as Resistance

Mappin's worldview is steeped in the canon of English letters, which has always doubled as a canon of resistance. Shakespeare captured the tension between power and legitimacy. His kings rise or fall by their words, their legitimacy tested not just on battlefields but in speeches. Mappin borrows this theatricality, speaking not as a bureaucrat but as a man who knows that politics is theatre, and theatre is truth-telling.

William Blake, mystic rebel, envisioned Albion as a fallen giant, enslaved by greed, reason, and the 'dark Satanic mills' of industrial modernity, but capable of awakening through imagination. Mappin channels this Blakian fire when he insists that Camelot is not just stone but symbol, a rebuke to the soulless machinery of modernity.

John Milton, revolutionary poet, thundered against censorship in *Areopagitica*: "Give me the liberty to know, to utter, and to argue freely according to conscience, above all liberties." Mappin could sign his name under that line today. His essays and interviews echo Milton's conviction that truth must be spoken even against the powers of state, science, or media.

G.K. Chesterton reminded a weary world that tradition is 'the democracy of the dead,' a way of giving our ancestors a vote. He saw modernity as absurd, a place where bureaucrats were revered and saints mocked. Mappin, with his dinner jackets, scripture quotes, and mischievous humour online, channels Chesterton's holy jester spirit.

Alfred, Lord Tennyson in *Idylls of the King* resurrected Arthur for the Victorian age, reminding a modernising nation that chivalry and myth were not quaint but vital. Camelot Castle is a continuation of that Arthurian revival. Not just nostalgia, but an assertion that Britain's story must be told again in every generation.

George Orwell warned of Newspeak and the destruction of truth by language itself. His vision of a state that polices speech to destroy thought is no longer fiction but daily news. Mappin invokes Orwell constantly, seeing in censorship and 'misinformation' policing the same disease Orwell diagnosed: tyranny through language.

And then there is T.S. Eliot, whose *Waste Land* depicted a civilisation fractured, barren, drained of meaning. 'These fragments I have shored against my ruins,' Eliot wrote. Mappin sees something similar in modern Britain. Fragments of culture without coherence, pieces of history without story. His task is to reweave them, to turn fragments into narrative again.

Mappin and the Restoration of Sanity

At its core, Mappin's project is about sanity. Not the psychiatric kind, with its pills and diagnoses, but the cultural kind. Coherence, continuity, meaning. A sane society is one that knows its story. An insane society is one that forgets.

Modern Britain risks madness because it has forgotten Albion. Its leaders speak in jargon, its culture is mediated by bureaucracy, its children are raised on algorithmic distraction rather than myth. Mappin refuses to accept this drift into amnesia. Through his writing, his oratory, and his staging of Camelot, he restores the memory of Albion.

Camelot Castle is not kitsch. It is a library in stone, a theatre in granite, a reminder that Britain is not a spreadsheet but a story. Within its walls, conversations happen that would be impossible elsewhere. Guests from across the spectrum sit at one table, echoing the Round Table's principle that no seat is higher than another. This, too, is sanity restored. Dialogue instead of division, story instead of slogans.

He often remarks that Camelot has seen actors, politicians, generals, and philosophers break bread at the same table. What matters is not their rank or their role, but their willingness to speak honestly. In this sense, Camelot is less a hotel than a Round Table reborn. It is theatre, hospitality, and philosophy fused together. It is Albion remembered in stone and speech.

He put it to me in words that linger: "Sanity is not the absence of pain. It is the presence of rational meaning." That aphorism is not clinical. It is literary and moral. It suggests that the path back to wholeness runs through story, and through truth told out loud, even when it hurts.

Optimism: Candles in the Ruins

For all the fire in his rhetoric, Mappin is not a prophet of doom. His vision is defiantly hopeful. He believes that Albion can awaken, that literature can rekindle imagination, that truth can outlast censorship.

History backs him up. Milton wrote in the shadow of censorship, yet his words live. Blake died in poverty, yet his verses now shape nations. Orwell warned in exile, yet his name has become shorthand for truth against tyranny. Words outlive empires. Stories outlast regimes. Albion, however wounded, can rise.

This is why Mappin insists on myth, poetry, and pageantry. They are not escapism, they are weapons of renewal. In an age of psychiatric sedation and technocratic decay, Camelot offers poetry, conversation, and conscience. In a world of lies, it offers the word and new ideas.

Here, optimism is not naïve. It is heroic. It is Blake's vision of Jerusalem built 'In England's green and pleasant land.' It is Tennyson's cry, 'To strive, to seek, to find, and not to yield.' It is Chesterton's paradoxical joy, Milton's liberty of conscience, Shakespeare's band of brothers. All echo in Mappin's creed.

He may never sit in Parliament, but in the strange, sacred theatre of this island's story, Mappin plays a role older than parties and deeper than policies. He is Albion's mythmaker, a man with a castle for a desk and a nation for a manuscript. He writes, he speaks, he stages, and in doing so, he calls Albion to wake once more.

The Restoration of Sanity, in the end, is not just political. It is literary. It is the recovery of Britain's story, spoken aloud and written afresh. And John Mappin, unconventional to some who seek to suppress his purpose, prophetic to others, is one of the few still holding the candle in the ruins, reminding us that the Word is not lost. Albion is not dead, and sanity can yet be restored.

CHAPTER NINE

The Hero's Anchor:
Mappin's Spiritual Conviction

T here is one aspect of mankind's relationship with religions and spiritual future on which Mappin is crystal clear.

"A dramatic revival and increasing interest in all religions is now occurring on this earth at a pace that we have never before seen."

"Millions have seen through the psychiatric program of materialism. They know it is a lie. They feel betrayed. They are reaching for understanding."

"They are reaching to understand their own spirituality and it is starting to dawn on many previously unconscious souls, that they might indeed be immortal and survive beyond the current life."

"The whole world is most certainly experiencing a hugely accelerated, tectonic and great awakening."

The hero is the one who steps voluntarily into chaos, sword in hand, not because he is certain of victory, but because he knows that without confrontation the dragon only grows. Yet beside the hero stands the watchman, the sentinel of order, whose role is to guard the walls, to see further, to hold the line so the hero has a world worth saving. These two archetypes dance in tension: the hero brings renewal through risk, the watchman brings continuity through vigilance.

But they are not alone. The great drama of being is populated by other figures. The king, who embodies order when justice and tyranny are corrupted, the trickster, who dissolves certainty so that new truths can emerge; and the sage, who carries wisdom distilled from the long past.

And beneath all these archetypes lies the same question: what anchors them?

The hero requires more than passing conviction or external approval; he requires the recognition that life itself is spiritual in nature, that awareness and will are not accidents of biology but the very essence of being. It is this certainty, that the individual is more than flesh and circumstance, which prevents the sword from becoming brittle and allows courage to endure.

John Mappin dances between and across these archetypes.

He is both hero and watchman.

"Individuals should be free to explore without interference." In expressing his view, Mappin aligns himself with a broader tradition of defending personal conscience as sacred.

He often points out the hypocrisy of those who preach tolerance for diversity of race, gender, or culture, but who mock or vilify religious minorities.

"To ridicule or criticise someone for their faith," he argues, "is no more enlightened than to deride them for their heritage or race."

True tolerance means permitting others to believe differently, to worship differently, and to live differently, without coercion or ridicule.

Mappin told me, "A sane or loving God or any rational being would not intend disagreements between religions or to see people using religion as the excuse for conflict or wars. Where this is occurring in the world one is always looking at manmade or synthetic factors that cause such enmities and generally a hidden profiteer."

A golden rule for living that is worth knowing well is to respect the religious beliefs of others.

Those who expect either evangelism or secrecy find instead an unembarrassed but non coercive viewpoint in Mappin: open to questions, honest about the role of all religions.

Individual Merit Above All

At the heart of Mappin's approach is an insistence on individual merit. He judges people by their actions, their character, and their willingness to stand for truth. Whatever religion a person is.

What matters is courage, honour, and personal integrity.

He says, "Any truly sane person first needs to be able to objectively see the factors within their own religious groups, religious leaders or religions that are less than ideal, irrespective of which religion, and they need to be able to have the willingness to self-inspect and to have the courage to correct those points in the service of life and mankind."

When we spoke on this subject Mappin referred me to two verses in the Christian Gospel

'Why do you look at the speck of sawdust in your brother's eye and pay no attention to the plank in your own eye? How can you say to your brother, "Let me take the speck out of your eye," when all the time there is a plank in your own eye? You hypocrite, first take the plank out of your own eye, and then you will see clearly to remove the speck from your brother's eye.'

Matthew 7:3–5 (NIV)

When stressing the importance of respecting the religious beliefs of others Mappin referred me to an often overlooked Surah of the Koran.

Surah Al-Kafirun (109:6)

لَكُمْ دِينِيكُمْ وَلِيَ دِينِ

'To you be your religion, and to me mine.'

A short, powerful declaration of mutual respect. Muslims follow their path, others follow theirs.

And again on the supremacy of the simplicity of truth over dogma he referred me to this Koranic Surah.

Surah Al-Baqarah (2:256)

لَا إِكْرَاهَ فِي الدِّينِ

'There is no compulsion in religion.
Truth stands out clear from error.'

This verse is often cited to show that belief must be voluntary - coercion is forbidden.

This is why his circle of friends is so eclectic, from traditional conservatives to radical reformers, from outspoken believers to equally outspoken critics of religion. Mappin can find common cause with anyone who refuses to bow to lies, regardless of creed. Many of his friends hold deeply Christian beliefs, with the late Charlie Kirk being one example and Candace and George Farmer another, as are Levantine leaders and eastern sages and leaders of thought who have found comfort, religious inspiration and sometimes insight in his company and he in theirs.

Often these individuals discover long lost unity in Mappin's orbit, and find his willingness to experience any view, rather an interesting additional dimension to their friend.

To write about John Mappin as a religious unifier of purpose is natural. It is simply true to recognise that for him, man's relationship with his understanding of himself and his immortal nature is one thread in the larger and extremely active tapestry of his life.

It influences him without defining him. It grounds him without imprisoning him. And it inspires him without compelling him to influence others.

The Extended Reflection

Just as he criticises psychiatry for attempting to define people by diagnostic labels, so too he resists the idea that any religion should define a person wholly.

It is not a dividing line between friend and stranger, ally and adversary, or worthy and unworthy.

Mappin's way of speaking about religion is disarmingly simple. He does not argue that others must accept it, nor does he seek to persuade. Instead, if asked, he extends an open invitation. Consider it, go to a church, mosque or temple, if you wish, read scripture or attend a lecture, if you feel inclined, or ignore it entirely if you so wish.

His message is not 'you must agree' but 'you are free to look.'

Mappin has no desire to convince the unwilling. His respect for conscience is too great, and his belief in individual sovereignty too central, to waste any energy on coercion.

In private conversations, he has been known to put it this way; if any philosophy or religion is true, it will withstand scrutiny. Truth does not need defence. Either way, the choice belongs to the individual, not to institutions, mobs, or media pundits.

One of Mappin's most consistent refrains is that labels, while convenient, rarely capture the truth of a person. Mappin himself refuses to do this with others.

In family life, in friendships, he seeks loyalty, honesty, and courage, not religious agreement.

In business, he values integrity and competence not religious identity. And in politics, where alliances often cut across ideological and religious boundaries, he has proven his ability to work with Christians, Muslims, Jewish people, Hindus, Sikhs, and atheists, or those of no faith at all.

To him, being religious neither sanctifies nor condemns. It is not a guarantee of virtue, nor a mark of vice.

At the heart of Mappin's approach is an insistence on individual merit. He judges people by their actions, their character, and their willingness to stand for truth. Mappin can find common cause with anyone who refuses to bow to lies, regardless of creed.

In this, Mappin's stance may be the most radical of all. For in a world that constantly seeks to label, divide, and categorise people on the basis of religion, he insists on something simpler: people first, labels last. Whether you share his view or not, you are welcome at his table.

And that, perhaps, is the truest reflection of his personal philosophy. Heroes test boundaries, wrestle with ideas that unsettle, and search for truths that polite society prefers to ignore.

If the restoration of sanity is this book's brief, then Mappin's stance offers a clue. Sanity is not conformity. Sanity is the courage to see with one's own eyes, to question, to doubt, and still to believe in the dignity of the individual. That is not merely a philosophy; it is the stuff of heroism. And yet heroism is never private. To live authentically is not only to free oneself but to set others free. That freedom calls for more than courage of character; it requires clarity of thought. It requires an intellect sharp enough to cut through illusion, deception, and the great lies of an age.

It requires, as Mappin puts it, 'the rehabilitation of the power of choice.' And perhaps that is the simplest expression of sovereignty that we have available today.

Is one self-determined, and does one have the power to choose in those areas of life where they believe they should be sovereign? When an individual is truly sovereign, they wield the sword of truth. It gleams like Excalibur in the mists of our confusion, waiting for the hand that dares to grasp it.

In the next part of this book it rises, a blade of light against the shadows, the weapon by which deception is broken and the path to freedom made clear.

PART FOUR

THE SWORD OF TRUTH

CHAPTER TEN

Mappin and the Philosopher's Fight for Sanity

The Philosopher Warrior

B eneath the patriot, beneath the media maverick, and beneath the firebrand cultural critic lies another side of John Mappin, the philosopher. Not in the academic sense, detached, abstract, locked in ivory towers, but in the classical sense, the seeker of truth, the challenger of assumptions, the one who dares to ask, "What is good?" and, "What is just?" even when the answer threatens the ruling orthodoxy.

Mappin's worldview has more in common with Socrates than with any modern politician. Like the Athenian gadfly, he refuses to accept the lies and euphemisms that grease the machinery of the state. He sees through the pretence, the polished PR, the moral gaslighting, and insists on returning to first principles. What is a nation? What is truth? What is freedom if it must be licensed by the government?

The Socratic Method in Cornwall

At the heart of Socrates' legacy is the Socratic method, not a doctrine but a discipline of relentless questioning. Socrates was feared not because he claimed to have answers, but because he exposed the ignorance of those who pretended to. Mappin, too, has made enemies not by shouting slogans, but by asking forbidden questions. Why were children masked? Why were critics of lockdown silenced? Why are our borders open while our citizens are told to tighten their belts? Why is free speech treated as a threat?

These are not gotchas. They are philosophical probes designed to pierce the veil of illusion. Mappin believes, as Socrates did, that a democracy without truth is just theatre. And a state that punishes dissent is not enlightened, it is insecure.

Philosophy as Leadership

From Plato, Mappin draws the idea of the philosopher king, not a literal monarch but a leader who governs not for power but with wisdom. A ruler who is shaped not by ambition but by duty. A man who would rather retreat than lie, but who steps forward when truth is under siege. Mappin's refusal to toe the establishment line, even when it costs him comfort or reputation, is rooted in this classical view of leadership. You do not serve yourself, you serve the ideal.

From Heraclitus, he echoes the belief that 'character is fate,' that the moral fibre of a man determines the course of his life. Mappin's character is one of inner discipline and defiant clarity. He does not posture for approval, nor does he retreat from confrontation. Like the Stoics, Epictetus, Marcus Aurelius, Seneca, he believes in personal responsibility, mastery of the self, and the importance of aligning one's actions with eternal truths, not passing trends.

And in the spirit of Diogenes, the most radical of the ancient philosophers, Mappin is willing to be laughed at, dismissed, or exiled from polite society in order to expose hypocrisy. Diogenes walked through Athens with a lantern, claiming to look for an honest man. Mappin walks through modern Britain with the same metaphorical light, searching not just for honesty, but for courage, integrity, and moral sanity in an age of doublethink.

His defiance of media spin, political correctness, and technocratic groupthink is not rebellion for its own sake. It is a form of philosophical hygiene, a refusal to allow falsehood to become law.

The Driving Force of History

Mappin has often argued that the true driving force of history is not armies, not economies, not even raw political power. It is philosophy. It is Ideas.

Behind every war or peace, every advance or collapse, lies a set of ideas that governs human action. If the ideas are rooted in truth and liberty, societies flourish. If they are poisoned by falsehood and coercion, societies descend into chaos.

This is not an abstraction for him. He points to history as a ledger of philosophies put into action. The Magna Carta, the Declaration of Independence, the Enlightenment, all of these were philosophical breakthroughs before they were political documents. They arose from ideas about liberty and reason, and in turn they gave rise to prosperity and stability. By contrast, when philosophy falters, peace falters. The French Revolution descended into terror because it lost its moorings in reason. The ideologies of communism and fascism rejected the sovereignty of the individual and substituted it with dogma, and the result was mass death.

Mappin sees the same struggle playing out today. Across the battlefields of Eastern Europe, in the culture wars of the West, in the censored platforms of the digital age, two philosophies clash. On one side stand those who prize truth, reason, and human dignity. On the other, those who peddle relativism, censorship, and control. This, in his view, is not a fight about policy detail. It is a struggle for the soul of civilisation itself.

That is why he writes and speaks with urgency. Philosophy is not an academic pursuit to him. It is life and death. Bad philosophy, he warns, is seductive, it offers easy answers, flatters emotion, and despises evidence. Good philosophy demands vigilance, courage, and clarity. The wars of tomorrow begin in the minds of men today. Ideas are the sparks that light battlefields or the lamps that preserve peace.

Camelot as Philosophy in Action

Camelot Castle has become his proof that philosophy must be lived, not merely spoken. There are moments, he insists, when an abstract principle must become a concrete act of defiance. His refusal to accept the Home Office's offer to turn Camelot Castle into migrant housing was one such moment.

On paper it looked like a routine administrative contract. But Mappin recognised that the decision carried a weight far beyond the walls of the hotel. To accept would be to allow a cultural landmark, bound up with the mythology of Arthur and Albion, to be quietly repurposed in service of a policy never put to the British people. To refuse would be to defend not just a building, but a principle, that heritage cannot be sold, that sovereignty cannot be bribed away.

He chose to refuse, and to speak openly about that refusal. In so doing he transformed what might have been a local administrative matter into a national and international story. His conversations with the mainstream press, Tucker Carlson, and GB News carried the story far beyond Cornwall. Millions saw the clips. Suddenly Britain's migrant hotel programme, once an unspoken bureaucratic routine, was laid bare as a national scandal.

For Mappin, this was philosophy in action. It was Socratic defiance applied to the modern world. Where others stayed silent, he asked the forbidden question, why are we being asked to surrender our heritage, and who gave government the right to do so? That question, once voiced, awakened a slumbering public. Towns and villages across Britain began to demand answers about what was happening in their communities.

Mappin has said many times that culture is not a side issue in politics. It is the heart of it. Symbols, archetypes, and stories shape the destiny of nations. To turn Camelot Castle into a holding depot would not only have harmed Tintagel's economy, it would have desecrated a national symbol. To resist was therefore not just a business decision but an act of cultural defence, one that reverberated across the country.

The Engineered Decline of Britain

From here, his Substack writings expand into what he sees as the deeper battle, the engineered decline of Britain. He argues that the crises of our time are not accidents of mismanagement but deliberate strategies of globalist ideology. Illegal migration, he insists, is not the result of incompetence but of policy. Britain's borders leak, its communities are transformed, and its sovereignty is eroded not because politicians are foolish, but because a class of bureaucrats and global institutions wishes it so.

This Deep State, as he calls it, is not a cabal of cartoon villains but a network of bureaucrats, corporate leaders, and political operatives who see nations as obstacles to their vision of global governance. In this vision, Britain is too strong, too independent, too steeped in heritage to be left alone. It must be softened, fragmented, and ultimately absorbed into supranational machinery.

For Mappin, this is not paranoia but pattern recognition. He cites history, empires weakened from within before they were conquered. Moral codes ridiculed. Patriotism painted as vice. Heritage denigrated until the people no longer knew who they were. He sees this same slow corrosion at work in Britain today, an education system stripped of pride, a media machine that labels dissent as extremism, and a culture so saturated in cynicism that it no longer remembers its own nobility.

The aim, he believes, is to separate the British from their heritage, to dissolve the bonds of loyalty to flag, family, and neighbour, until sovereignty can be surrendered without resistance. Migration on a mass scale is one weapon in this arsenal. Debt, dependency, and creeping regulation are others. Each crisis becomes a pretext for further centralisation, each outrage an excuse to erode liberty.

Mappin's warning is stark, sovereignty, once lost, is not easily reclaimed. But he couples that warning with a call to lawful and peaceful resistance. Violence, he insists, would only feed the very system he opposes. Britain's defence must come through its ancient liberties, speech, debate, conscience, and civic action. He writes often that the British people have survived worse than this, blitz, famine, invasion, and that improbable comebacks are part of their story. What the globalists fear most, he argues, is not a mob but a people awake, articulate, and unafraid.

The Philosopher Warrior Archetype

Taken together, these philosophical threads form a coherent vision. Ideas determine the fate of nations. Bad philosophy leads to decline and war. Good philosophy, rooted in truth and liberty, preserves peace. But philosophy must be lived, not just thought. The refusal at Camelot was philosophy incarnate. And the broader struggle against engineered decline is a battle of ideas as much as borders.

Mappin therefore positions himself, not as a politician chasing office, but as a philosopher warrior in the classical mould. His Substack, his media appearances, his Round Tables at Camelot Castle, all serve one purpose, to defend truth, to awaken conscience, and to restore sanity in an age of engineered madness.

Britain at the Crossroads

Britain, he insists, stands at a crossroads. To choose truth, sovereignty, and sanity is to choose survival. To choose falsehood, coercion, and apathy is to choose decline. The task of philosophy is to illuminate that choice and to remind the nation of its soul.

And yet, John Mappin's vision does not stop at Britain's borders. The restoration of sanity is not merely a domestic duty, it is a global necessity. Wars, hoaxes, and psychological manipulations spill across frontiers, the lies of Westminster and Brussels become the crises of Kyiv and Cornwall. If truth is the first casualty of war, then it is also the first requirement of peace.

Which is why, in the next movement of his story, Mappin steps into a role that few could have imagined for him, not only the philosopher warrior of Camelot, but the intermediary, the convener, the man who dares to build bridges where governments burn them. Camelot itself, perched on the Cornish cliffs, becomes more than a symbol. It becomes a living Round Table, a meeting ground where sanity challenges hysteria, and where the possibility of peace can be kept alive in an age drunk on war.

It is here that the story turns outward, from Cornwall to the capitals of the world. And it is here that John Mappin's defiance of deception becomes something greater still. An effort to avert global conflict itself.

Averting Global Conflict

The Hero's Task

Every culture has known that the greatest danger to civilisation is not only the enemy beyond the walls but the chaos that festers within them. The hero archetype emerges in precisely such times, when catastrophe seems inevitable and when only courage, clarity, and sacrifice can turn the tide. To avert global conflict is not the work of accountants or bureaucrats. It is the work of the hero who dares to confront dragons before they devour whole nations.

Yet the hero never stands alone. Behind him lies the community he defends, the walls that must hold, the future that must not collapse. In the old stories, the knight goes forth not because victory is certain, but because the alternative is unthinkable. He faces the abyss because only by facing it can the abyss be pushed back.

Our world teeters at such an edge. Global conflict whispers at the margins of every crisis. Economic collapse, cultural fragmentation, ideological warfare. Each threatens to cascade into catastrophe if left unchecked. But the heroic path begins with responsibility: the willingness of one person to shoulder the burden when others look away.

To understand John Mappin's role here is to see him as a man inhabiting the archetype of the sentinel-hero. One who steps forward to name the danger, to connect the dots, and to hold the line so that others may still have a future to inherit.

Lies That Lit the Fire, Truth That Can End It

Once upon a time, Barack Obama was sold to the West as a messianic figure. A man of grace, eloquence, and moral clarity. The 'hope and change' president. The globalist's poster boy. But behind the soft lighting and teleprompter poetry lurked something else, something far darker. As John Mappin rightly points out in his meticulous takedown of the so-called 'Russia Hoax,' Obama wasn't just a spectator of one of the greatest political frauds in modern history, he was its architect.

The Russia Hoax, in case you've mercifully forgotten, was the years-long media and intelligence campaign to convince the world that Donald J. Trump was a Kremlin asset, a Manchurian candidate hand-picked by Vladimir Putin to destroy American democracy from within. The claim was absurd from the start, yet it consumed public discourse, cost millions in taxpayer funds, led to illegal surveillance of U.S. citizens, and crippled the first three years of Trump's presidency. It divided nations, wrecked reputations, and became gospel truth in every Guardian op-ed and BBC panel show.

But it was all a lie. Fabricated. Orchestrated. Weaponised. And at the centre of it all? Barack Hussein Obama.

Mappin has long argued that Russiagate was never about Russia. It was about control. About ensuring that the populist revolution ignited by Trump, mirrored in Brexit and other nationalist awakenings, was suffocated before it could challenge the permanent ruling class. Mappin was mocked for saying it, but time has vindicated him. Declassified memos, Senate reports, the Durham investigation, all confirm that this wasn't a case of intelligence failure. It was a case of intelligence weaponisation. And it all traces back to the Obama White House.

It was under Obama that intelligence agencies, once forbidden from domestic political interference, were unleashed against political opponents. It was Obama's team that briefed then-Vice President Biden on efforts to frame General Michael Flynn. It was Obama's CIA chief John Brennan and FBI director James Comey who knowingly ran with the Steele dossier, a document so riddled with fiction it would make Ian Fleming blush. And let's not forget the 'insurance policy,' Peter Strzok's smug text message, assuring his lover Lisa Page that the Deep State had a plan to derail Trump's candidacy should democracy do something inconvenient, like elect him.

Obama didn't just tolerate this machinery, he activated it. He knew. He was briefed. And, if we're honest, it was all perfectly in character. This was never the 'post-partisan' president. This was a man who weaponised the IRS against conservative groups. Who spied on journalists. Who oversaw drone assassinations while collecting Nobel Peace Prizes. The global media sold him as Moses. In reality, he was Machiavelli with better lighting.

What Mappin understood early, well before it was safe or fashionable to say so, was that this wasn't just an American scandal. It was a global ideological operation. The Russia narrative was deployed in Britain, too, used to discredit Brexit campaigners, smear Nigel Farage, and justify further censorship and surveillance of dissident voices. To question mass immigration? Russian influence. To challenge climate alarmism? Russian bot. To support national sovereignty over supranational control? Clearly, you're a puppet of Putin. It was Orwellian, but slick. And it all worked, until it didn't.

As the truth continues to leak out, the legacy of Obama is being quietly rewritten, not by the media, of course, but by facts. Cold, uncomfortable, undeniable facts. The man who promised transparency presided over a political spying campaign. The constitutional law professor shredded constitutional norms. And the great peacemaker laid the groundwork for a new Cold War, against his own citizens.

Millions of decent people bought into it. They watched the BBC and CNN, read the Guardian and the New York Times, and genuinely believed that the populist right had been infiltrated by Russian saboteurs. They dismissed anyone who challenged the narrative as conspiracy theorists, traitors, or 'far-right extremists.' They didn't realise they were the ones being manipulated, gaslit by the very institutions they trusted most.

Mappin's warning was simple: don't confuse appearance with virtue. Don't confuse smooth speech with honest leadership. And don't for a second believe that Western democracies are immune to the kinds of state-sponsored deception we so often attribute to far-off dictatorships. The danger to liberty isn't always external, it's often right at the centre of power, speaking in full sentences and wearing a Nobel medal.

The Hoax as Detonator

For Mappin, Russiagate was not just a partisan scandal. It was geopolitical vandalism. The hoax poisoned the very possibility of diplomacy with Russia. Every attempt at détente by Trump was met with accusations of treachery. Every handshake was portrayed as betrayal. The mere act of speaking rationally and reasonably about reducing conflict and working towards peace became politically suicidal.

This was by design. As Mappin describes it, the hoax, "Paved the road to war." It shackled Trump, consumed his presidency, and taught an entire generation of Western politicians that peace with Russia was not only unfashionable but forbidden. That prohibition led directly to the tragedy of Ukraine.

However, the war did not begin in Donbas, nor in the Kremlin's gilded halls, nor even in Kyiv. Its origins lie many years before in Washington, London, and Brussels. It was seeded by intelligence agencies, fertilised by media hysteria, and harvested by a political class desperate to maintain its grip on power.

And the price has been catastrophic. Over one and half million dead or maimed. Millions more displaced. Cities reduced to rubble. European economies shattered by energy crises. American taxpayers bled for $175 billion and counting. Trillions of dollars drained from global GDP. A hoax metastasised into mass death.

The beneficiaries? Energy conglomerates with record profits, arms manufacturers whose share prices soared, media outlets selling propaganda as readily as they once sold Russiagate, and political elites who use war as cover for failure. For them, carnage is currency.

History, Mappin insists, must record this clearly. The Ukraine war was not born of inevitability, but of lies. Those who seeded Russiagate were not merely playing politics. They were laying kindling for a conflagration that would consume nations.

The Theatre of Weakness

The war has been stage-managed as much as fought. Mappin points to one particular spectacle, Zelensky's visit to Washington, flanked by a parade of European leaders. The press called it unity. In reality, it was dependency dressed as grandeur.

Why, Mappin asked, does a sovereign leader need half of Europe to trail behind him like nervous stagehands? Because he is not sovereign. He is a frontman. The real decision makers are not in Kyiv but in Washington,

Brussels, and the boardrooms of defence contractors.

The optics gave the game away. Strong nations do not need entourages to project confidence. The photo-op was less Churchill in the Blitz and more a quarterly shareholders' meeting, with Zelensky as the presenter and the Western elites as the investors, checking their balance sheets.

For Mappin, the image symbolised Europe's weakness. Once nations of independence, they now shuffle behind Washington, terrified of their own citizens' wrath, desperate to spread the blame thin. What was sold as solidarity was in fact theatre, the choreography of a managed war.

The Merchants of Perpetual War

And behind the theatre lies the addiction. Mappin's words are unflinching. War is their narcotic. The arms barons, the oil majors, the grain speculators, all are vampires feeding on blood and ruin. Every missile launched, every bomb dropped, is another hit of profit.

Since the invasion of Ukraine, energy giants have feasted on volatility, raking in $380 billion in just two years. Defence contractors soared on stock markets. Food traders turned crises into cash. This is not capitalism. It is cannibalism.

So when rumours swirl of Trump and Putin circling a peace summit, when the faint scent of peace is in the air, the addicts panic. They smear peace as appeasement. They flood the airwaves with propaganda. And when that fails, they reach for sabotage; terror attacks, false flags, assassinations, anything to keep the war drug flowing.

For these merchants of death, peace is withdrawal. And withdrawal is agony. That is why, Mappin warns, they will stop at nothing to keep the killing going.

Psychiatry and the Philosophy of Control

Yet Mappin insists that the roots run even deeper. Behind every lie, behind every inversion of truth, he sees the hand of psychiatry, not as medicine, but as philosophy. Psychiatry, in his view, is the intellectual skeleton of deception. It reduces man to a machine, denies spirit, pathologises dissent, and turns disagreement into disease.

The Russia Hoax, he argues, bore all the hallmarks of such a psychiatric operation: obsessive repetition, gaslighting, the pathologising of those who disbelieved. The message was hammered relentlessly, designed not to persuade with reason, but to condition with fear. Doubt was treated as illness. Questioning the narrative was branded as extremism. Whole populations were nudged into compliance as though they were patients in need of treatment rather than citizens with minds of their own.

In this sense, Russiagate was not just politics, it was a test case. It was a demonstration of how entire nations could be medicated with lies, their civic will sedated by narratives as potent as drugs. Tulsi Gabbard's disclosures confirmed this much, pointing to the Obama administration's deliberate use of psychological conditioning to reinforce the hoax. To Mappin, this was not coincidence, but the clear imprint of psychiatry. The weaponisation of the human mind against itself.

And the consequences were global. The psychiatric inversion of truth. Trump framed as delusional. Russia demonised as the inevitable enemy became the ideological alibi for the Ukraine war. A deception metastasised into carnage.

For Mappin, psychiatry is the perfect tool for tyranny. It teaches that truth is subjective, conscience irrelevant, and freedom a disorder. It is the philosophy that undergirds censorship, medical coercion, and endless war. Unless it is exposed and rejected, nations cannot reclaim their sanity or their sovereignty.

Camelot as Counter-Symbol

And so, against the hoaxes, the theatre, the addictions, and the deceptions, John Mappin offers something different. Camelot.

Not simply a castle on the cliffs, but a symbol. A Round Table where leaders can meet not as puppets of Brussels or Washington, but as men and women of conscience. A place rooted in myth and heritage, standing in defiance of the psychiatric worldview that reduces man to machine.

Camelot is Mappin's counter to Davos. Where the World Economic Forum plots control, Camelot offers freedom. Where NATO summits choreograph dependency, Camelot invites sovereignty. Where media spins theatre, Camelot insists on truth.

In a world stumbling toward great power conflict, Mappin casts himself not as a king but as a convener. His vision is of Britain reclaiming its role as honest broker, not lapdog. Camelot as intermediary nexus, not for war profiteers, but for truth seekers. A Round Table, not for knights of myth, but for leaders willing to speak plainly about peace.

The symbolism matters. Against the sterile conference halls of Brussels, Camelot stands as a beacon. Against the grey technocracy of globalist forums, it offers colour, story, legend. Mappin knows that politics is never just about policies, it is about imagination. And Camelot, in all its mythic resonance, gives the imagination of peace a home.

The Verdict of History

History may yet record the Ukraine war not only as a tragedy of blood and rubble, but as the most preventable conflict of the modern age. It did not have to happen. It happened because lies triumphed over truth, because theatre triumphed over sovereignty, because addicts of war triumphed over the will of ordinary people.

Mappin's warning is simple, but urgent. If the world continues to allow hoaxes, psychiatric deceptions, and profiteers to dictate policy, conflict is inevitable. But if truth, sovereignty, and conscience are restored, peace is possible.

Putin's remark, that the war would never have begun under Trump, is not propaganda. It is a sober reflection of cause and effect. And it is the vindication of what Mappin has said all along, wars begin in the minds of men, and only truth can avert them.

The question now is whether Camelot, with its mythic resonance and its living Round Table, can serve as a counterweight to the warmongers. Whether leaders will choose truth over theatre. Whether the faint scent of peace, so terrifying to profiteers, will be allowed to become reality.

Because if not, if the merchants of perpetual war prevail, if psychiatry's deceptions remain unchallenged, then the world will stumble again into darkness, and the chance for peace will be lost.

Mappin's task, then, is not merely commentary. It is guardianship. To guard truth against lies, sanity against psychiatry, sovereignty against globalism. To remind leaders, and nations, that peace is not weakness, but wisdom. And in that task, Camelot is a beacon.

A Diplomat in All but Name

Over the course of researching and writing this book, I have been privileged to speak with people of considerable influence, individuals whose words carry weight in the highest circles of politics, business, and global affairs. More than once, and from more than one country, I have been told with quiet certainty that John Mappin has played a direct role in brokering conversations, opening back channels, and facilitating dialogue at moments of genuine geopolitical tension.

It is important to be clear about what this means. Mappin is not tied to any single party or ideology. He has moved across the political spectrum and across borders with the same insistence on conscience and truth that defines his public voice. Some of the subjects he has been involved with are too politically sensitive to discuss openly; others remain confidential for obvious reasons. But the fact of his involvement is undeniable.

I have had the rare privilege of glimpsing some of this first hand. I have seen written exchanges and heard in-person discussions that leave no doubt about the seriousness with which he is regarded in certain quarters. I have sat in the same room as Mappin while he was in active dialogue with senior American diplomatic contacts and high-ranking British politicians. I have seen enough, and heard enough, to know that his role is real, even if much of it will never be public.

True to his nature, he does not boast about these encounters. Rather, he is quintessentially English in his approach, discreet, understated, more inclined to see himself as a small part of a larger mechanism than as the centre of the story. He describes himself as one cog in a wheel, a contributor to a process that allows conversations to happen where official channels falter. The political establishment, with its rituals and protocols, is too often paralysed, too antiquated, too compromised, too prejudiced, or simply too slow to act when history demands imagination and courage. Camelot, by contrast, has become a space where dialogue is possible, where leaders can meet not as adversaries across a negotiating table, but as human beings in search of solutions.

There are moments in history when official diplomacy falters, and it is individuals outside the machinery of state who hold open the space for peace, however fragile. Mappin has been such a figure. A philosopher-diplomat, working without title or office, yet enabling encounters that matter. Out of respect for those involved, I will not disclose more than has been permitted. But I can say this, his Round Table is not metaphorical alone. It is a working reality, and it has already made its quiet mark on the history of our time.

CHAPTER TWELVE

From Magna Carta to Camelot: The British Spirit of Free Speech

Tintagel and the Mythic Quest

The oath sworn at Runnymede, the fire carried by Milton, the warning thundered by Orwell; these are all chapters in the same story. Britain's struggle to defend liberty against the powers that would smother it. At Camelot, that lineage is not merely remembered but lived. The myths of Arthur and the Round Table find a modern counterpart in the defence of conscience and the refusal to bow to orthodoxy.

To stand on Tintagel's cliffs is to feel that myth is never far from history. Below, the Atlantic hammers the rock as it has for a thousand years; above, the ruins of Arthur's castle brood against the horizon. For centuries this headland has been a place where story and sovereignty meet. Arthur's Round Table, whether fact or fable, symbolised equality of voice, the idea that no one man sits above the others. Britain itself can be seen as an island Round Table, a nation that, at its best, invited its people to speak without fear. Mappin, in his own way, has cast himself not as the author of a new myth but as the custodian of an old one, carrying forward a quest that began long before his time.

Magna Carta and the Line of Liberty

The inheritance he invokes can be traced back to that meadow in 1215, when King John was compelled to seal Magna Carta. It did not explicitly mention free speech, yet its words carried the force of rebellion: 'To no one will we sell to no one deny or delay right or justice.' This was not merely a legal contract but the planting of a principle. The law must curb the ruler, and conscience must not be silenced by decree. That principle, born on English soil, travelled far. It inspired the Petition of Right in 1628, echoed in the debates of the Civil War, and crossed the Atlantic to shape America's Bill of Rights. The idea that rulers must be bound and citizens free became the lodestar of the English-speaking world.

Milton gave that spirit new thunder. His defiance of censorship lit fires beyond his own century. Enlightenment thinkers on the Continent cited him as proof that conscience must stand higher than control. Voltaire, Locke, Jefferson, all drank from Milton's well. As Mappin reminded me, "The right to speak your conscience isn't just a British quirk, it became the foundation of the free world."

The Glorious Revolution of 1688 and the Bill of Rights enshrined robust debate in Parliament, but Mappin sees the duty as far wider. "If you can't say what you think, you aren't free," he told me. "And Britain is built on the idea that freedom is more important than comfort."

John Stuart Mill's *On Liberty* of 1859 carried the tradition forward, declaring that to silence an opinion was to 'rob the human race.' His words galvanised reformers, suffragettes, and dissenters in the industrial age. Mappin admires Mill precisely because he warned that silencing even a lone eccentric robs everyone of truth. "Censorship isn't a mistake," he said to me. "It's a betrayal of who we are as a people."

Like Orwell, he fears the tyranny of euphemism and groupthink; like Churchill, he knows that liberty is tested not by defending the easy opinion but the dangerous one.

From Runnymede to Orwell, the British tradition of liberty has always doubled as a restoration of sanity against the delirium of unchecked power. To silence truth is to unhinge the mind of a nation; to speak it is to restore the balance. Every age has had its madness; the tyranny of kings, the fever of ideology, the intoxication of empire, and in each case, it was the liberty to speak that began the cure.

The Bolshevik Warning

History teaches that suppression often cloaks itself in benevolence. Few regimes proved this more chillingly than the Soviet Union. There, dissent was not argued with, it was diagnosed. Opposition became pathology, and to question the regime was to be declared unwell. Psychiatry, rather than protecting the vulnerable, became a scalpel for political control.

Alexander Bogdanov, physician and revolutionary, epitomised this fusion of ideology and science. He taught that the soul was not divine but mechanical, a set of conditioned impulses ready to be re-educated. In his science-fiction novel *Red Star*, a communist Martian society sustains itself through literal blood transfusion. He experimented with the same idea in life and died in the process, convinced that man could be engineered. Trotsky, too, flirted with psychiatry, embracing Freud as a tool for decoding class struggle. By the 1930s Freud was discarded as bourgeois and replaced by Pavlov, whose salivating dogs became the model for human behaviour. Reflex theory became state doctrine: men and women were programmable, pliant, subject to the same conditioning as animals.

This was not science but sorcery in white coats. Soviet psychiatrists like Bekhterev and Kazhinsky even claimed telepathy could be explained mechanically, as if thoughts were radio signals. Others, like Aleksei Gastev, applied 'scientific management' to the very minds of workers, demanding that thoughts be regulated as precisely as muscle movements. Out of this infernal laboratory emerged the 'New Soviet Man,' obedient, collectivised, emptied of individuality. The Gulag was terrifying enough, but psychiatric wards became gulags of the mind. Dissenters were diagnosed with 'sluggish schizophrenia' and subjected to chemical restraint, electroshock, and the erasure of self.

Some saw the madness early. In 1919, the American journalist John Spargo called Bolshevism a mass psychosis. The Russian philosopher Nikolai Berdyaev remarked that Bogdanov interrogated ideas not as arguments but as symptoms. Truth itself had been sectioned.

For Mappin, the lesson is stark. Bolshevism was not born in the clinic, but psychiatry gave it a weapon more insidious than bullets. It allowed tyranny to masquerade as medicine, coercion as cure.

Cancel Culture as Soft Authoritarianism

Mappin pointed out to me that this legacy should not be filed away as distant history. "It's the same weapon today," he warned. "They just use new labels." What was once sluggish schizophrenia is now misinformation or radicalisation. The details differ, but the trick is the same: redefine conscience as sickness.

Cancel culture, in his eyes, is Bolshevism in softer clothing. Speech that challenges orthodoxy is not engaged, it is diagnosed. Social platforms sanitise discourse; trust and safety boards act as commissars; algorithms quietly exile voices from the public square. "The language is softer now," he told me, "but the effect is the same: compliance."

The Covid years proved how quickly Britain could slide into this pattern. Doctors who questioned lockdowns, parents who resisted school closures, and journalists who challenged mandates were branded cranks, paranoids, or 'anti-science.' Each epithet worked like a diagnosis, an excuse to dismiss rather than debate. "How many times did we hear the words misinformed or denier?" he asked me. "That's exactly the Soviet playbook. Turn dissent into disorder."

In the Covid years, when parents worried for their children and doctors questioned edicts, it was not they who had lost their sanity but the institutions that silenced them. To restore free speech now is therefore not merely to defend liberty, but to restore sanity to the nation. The refusal to hear dissent was itself the mark of a culture unmoored from reason, and the voices cast out as cranks often proved to be the only sane ones left in the room.

The danger grows sharper still when censorship curdles into violence. The chapter on Charlie Kirk showed the fatal end of this descent, a man murdered for nothing more than holding opinions that his opponents despised. That is where the culture of silencing leads when it mutates unchecked. From cancellation to intimidation, from intimidation to blood. The radical left has often excused this logic by branding speech itself as violence, but in doing so they invited real violence into the arena. To kill a man rather than debate him is the ultimate confession that you have no argument left. It is insanity masquerading as politics. And it is not only the left that carries this poison. Extremism on the right, too, turns dissent into a pretext for force. In both cases the result is the same. Words are replaced by weapons, dialogue by death.

Mappin insists that the only antidote is a culture where everyone, regardless of their opinion, is permitted to speak. For so long as people can argue, the literal sword need not be drawn. Silence enforced by violence is the surest mark of a civilisation losing its mind.

What psychiatry once offered the Bolsheviks, modern technocracy now offers through digital platforms. 'Misinformation' has become the new sluggish schizophrenia, a vague and infinitely malleable term that permits authorities to silence without ever admitting they fear the words themselves. And like the Soviet wards, today's digital gulags are quiet, bureaucratic, bloodless. A person disappears from the platform, their words erased, their audience dissolved. No bars are needed. Exile is just one click away.

Camelot as Bastion

Mappin warns that this is not merely a matter of convenience or corporate policy but a profound redefinition of what it means to be human. For if the soul is not permitted to speak, it is treated as defective. A man or woman silenced for conscience is not simply censored, they are pathologised. The message is clear, to resist is to be sick, to question is to be unstable, to disagree is to be dangerous.

This is why he insists that Camelot is more than a hotel. It is a counterweight to psychiatric authoritarianism, a place where those written off as mad elsewhere are given the dignity of being heard. What society calls unhinged may, in truth, be sanity refusing to bow. In giving those voices a seat at the Round Table, Mappin is not merely being provocative. He is reminding Britain that liberty depends on listening even to those whom the age despises. Especially to them.

Mappin's stance places him in a lineage of iconoclastic British dissenters. The Levellers demanded liberty of conscience against both crown and Parliament. The pamphleteers of Fleet Street skewered the powerful. Orwell dissected the instinct to make lies sound truthful and murder respectable. Churchill thundered that liberty was worth defending even when it gave offence.

Today, cultural figures like Rowan Atkinson and Ricky Gervais continue that lineage, reminding us that offence is not harm and truth is not hate. "The hated voice," Mappin told me, "is the test of whether you believe in liberty at all."

Camelot, then, is a gathering place where conscience is spoken aloud. Voices admired and despised alike find a seat. Liberty is not proven by indulging the popular view but by defending the outcast one. Mappin contrasted it to me with Davos: "They gather to manufacture consensus. We gather to break it open."

For him, Camelot is not a retreat from the world but a training ground for the battles that lie ahead. Within its walls, guests rediscover that offence is not fatal, that speaking one's mind is not madness but sanity. Each leaves emboldened, carrying fragments of liberty back into the bloodstream of the nation.

The Soul of Liberty

From Runnymede to Milton, from Mill to Orwell, from Churchill to Camelot, the spirit of liberty has always been tested by those who would silence it. The Bolsheviks remind us how swiftly dissent can be recast as disease. Cancel culture shows how quickly liberty can be sacrificed in the name of safety.

Britain did not fight tyrants for centuries only to be policed by hashtags and algorithms. Magna Carta was not sealed so Silicon Valley could issue licences for speech. Milton did not thunder against licensing so that conscience could be treated as pathology. "Take away a man's property and he may rebuild," Mappin told me. "Take away his voice and he cannot resist at all."

Without speech, madness becomes the law; with speech, even the most broken society can find its bearings again. That is why liberty is not a luxury but the last defence of sanity itself. Camelot stands as a reminder that free speech is not only the guardian of conscience but the cure for collective delirium. In giving words back to the silenced, it restores not just liberty, but sanity itself.

Britain now faces storms no less fierce than those that battered Tintagel's cliffs for centuries: globalist designs, digital censorship, the creeping psychiatric state. Yet the tradition of liberty has always been renewed in unlikely places: fields, taverns, pamphlet presses, and now a castle at the edge of the Atlantic.

Mappin does not claim to be a hero. He sees himself as a custodian, one cog in a greater wheel. Yet history often turns on such figures, those who refuse to conform, who hold open a space for freedom when the world insists it must close. The story of liberty is never finished. It is written anew in every age, defended by those willing to risk ridicule for truth. The flame is fragile but unextinguished.

Toward a Transatlantic Stage

Camelot, then, is not just a bastion for Britain but a lighthouse for the wider world. The same flame that flickered at Runnymede, which burned through Milton, Mill, and Orwell, now throws its light across the Atlantic. For Mappin, the defence of liberty is not parochial. It is part of a much larger contest: a battle over the future shape of civilisation itself.

He reminded me that Britain has never been an island unto itself. Our ideas have always crossed oceans. Just as Magna Carta inspired America's founding fathers, just as Churchill and Roosevelt forged the special relationship, Mappin believes that today's struggle for free speech and sovereignty must be transatlantic in scope. Cancel culture, financial coercion, and globalist conformity are not uniquely British ailments; they are symptoms of a crisis shared across the West.

Tintagel's cliffs may root him in Cornish granite, but his gaze is fixed on Washington, New York, and beyond. In his conversations with senators, broadcasters, and campaigners, he carries the same message that echoes through Camelot. Truth must be spoken, even when it destabilises the powerful. In that sense, Camelot has become a listening post on the edge of the Atlantic, tuned not only to Britain's heartbeat but to the tremors of a world in flux.

And so the quest continues, not only in the defence of liberty at home but in the great reordering abroad. For Mappin, the same principles that guard free speech in Cornwall also illuminate the decline of the dollar, the rise of BRICS, and the fragility of American power. To tell the story of Camelot is therefore to tell the story of a civilisation at a crossroads. A story that cannot be confined to Britain alone.

CHAPTER THIRTEEN

Camelot and the Reckoning of Empires

Bridges Across a Breaking World

Mappin is not a parochial figure bound by the borders of Britain. His reach extends far beyond Westminster or Whitehall. He is in constant dialogue with American legislators, media firebrands, and cultural influencers. For many across the Atlantic, Camelot Castle has become not merely a Cornish landmark but a listening post for the tides of global change. When Mappin writes or speaks, his audience is not only British; it is transatlantic. And his commentary on BRICS and the decline of the dollar is just one example of how he places Britain's fate within the larger drama of a world in flux.

When Mappin writes about geopolitics, he does so with a mixture of blunt clarity and historical sweep. In his July 2025 Infinite Futures Substack article, he turned his gaze to one of the most significant shifts in the global order: the rise of BRICS and the waning of American financial dominance. His argument was as provocative as it was precise. The BRICS surge isn't a plot against the United States; it is the natural result of America's own self-destruction.

"In the grand chessboard of global affairs, where the illusion of control is often more potent than control itself," Mappin begins, "a new configuration is forming - and it did not emerge from conquest. It was conjured into being by American negligence."

BRICS (originally Brazil, Russia, India, China, and South Africa) has expanded to include Egypt, Ethiopia, Iran, the UAE, and Saudi Arabia. To many in the Western press, it looks like an anti-Western bloc, a challenger to the so-called rules-based international order. But Mappin is quick to dismantle that narrative. "This is not a dagger aimed at the heart of the dollar," he writes. "It is the natural immune response of a world exhausted by Washington's moral hypocrisy, fiscal vandalism, and geopolitical recklessness."

The Weaponised Dollar

For Mappin, the dollar's decline began long before BRICS gained momentum. "Once a symbol of trust, of financial prudence, and American enterprise, it is now a battered totem wielded like a cudgel." He points to decades of, "Quantitative easing, deficit orgies, and economic myopia," as the root cause of the currency's erosion.

The dollar, he argues, has been 'weaponised' through sanctions on Russia, Iran, and even on supposed allies. "What rational actor would continue to peg its sovereignty to a financial system that punishes independence and rewards compliance with a decaying hegemon?" His conclusion is as concise as it is damning: "De-dollarisation is not rebellion; it is insurance."

From Proxy Wars to Realignment

Mappin traces the geopolitical realignment not to the BRICS expansion, but to decades of disastrous foreign interventions. "It began with Iraq. With Libya. With Afghanistan. With every airstrike that 'spread democracy' and every treaty shredded in the name of national security."

Each misstep eroded trust in American leadership. "The very nations that once looked to the U.S. for leadership now look to one another for escape. BRICS, then, is not a revolution - it is a lifeboat. And it is filling fast."

The war in Ukraine, in his view, only accelerated the shift. He lays part of the blame squarely on NATO's eastward push and, "The CIA's long flirtation with Kiev's corridors." Billions in Western aid and weaponry, he argues, have, "Not secured peace, but prolonged bloodshed. And the world is watching. Watching and calculating."

The Mirror America Will Not Face

For Mappin, the crisis is not just about foreign policy, it is about the philosophy driving it. "At the heart of this geopolitical decay is not merely bad policy - it is a rotten philosophy. A belief that America's role is to instruct rather than to listen. To dominate rather than to partner. To convert rather than to coexist."

He describes this as a fusion of, "Wilsonian missionary zeal," and "neocon imperial arrogance," creating, "an empire that cannot stop expanding, even as it collapses from within." The symptoms are visible at home - cultural division, crippling debt, politicised institutions - and they feed the perception abroad that America's power is as hollow as its currency.

"It is not that the world is abandoning the dollar," he warns, "it is that the dollar, and the empire behind it, have abandoned the world."

Multipolarity Is Not the Threat. It's the Cure.

While Washington frames BRICS as a danger to stability, Mappin sees it differently. "The rise of BRICS should not be feared. It should be understood. It signals not the end of the world, but the end of a monopoly."

He paints a picture of a new, multipolar world: one where Cairo speaks with Riyadh, where Delhi does not take instruction from Brussels, and where trade routes stretch from Vladivostok to Cape Town, perhaps, if America does not abandon their existing addiction to psychiatric philosophy, bypassing Washington altogether.

The Real Battle Is Within

Mappin's conclusion is both a warning and a challenge to America. "If America wishes to remain relevant in the coming age, it must first look inward. It must abandon the illusion that the rest of the world exists to prop up its comfort. It must slash its debt, temper its interventions, and restore the civic and spiritual foundations that once made it not feared, but admired."

Until that happens, BRICS will grow, "Not as an enemy force, but as a reflection of America's own decline. For no empire is destroyed from without. It dies when it can no longer recognise itself in the mirror."

Mappin's analysis is not just an economic commentary, it is a political obituary. He sees the fall of dollar dominance as less an act of sabotage than a slow suicide, committed in plain sight by a nation unwilling to change course.

In his telling, BRICS is not the villain of the story. It is simply the opportunist stepping into a vacuum left by a superpower too distracted, too arrogant, and too indebted to maintain the system it built. Whether one agrees with his conclusions or not, Mappin's framing forces a difficult question: is the West losing because others are winning, or because it no longer knows how to play?

The Transatlantic Connection

This is where Mappin's warm US friendships become crucial. Mappin and Tucker Carlson exchange insights that flow across the Atlantic. Whereas Carlson, unshackled from corporate media, has become the blunt instrument of truth in America, Mappin, from Camelot in Britain, resonates with a harmonic that achieves the same. Both men speak a language the establishment loathes. The language of candour.

Carlson's fearless exposés, from the failures of U.S. foreign policy to the scandals of Epstein, mirror Mappin's warnings about Western decline. Both insist that endless wars, financial vandalism, and cultural corrosion are not accidents, but the predictable outcomes of a corrupted ruling class. Where Mappin dissects the global chessboard, Carlson electrifies the American grassroots and Tucker's own geopolitical sphere.

Their synergy is powerful. When Carlson declared that Epstein's blackmail ring was tied to foreign intelligence, he shocked polite society but won cheers from the crowd. When Mappin declared that BRICS was not America's enemy but America's mirror, he forced his readers to confront the uncomfortable truth. Together, they represent a transatlantic axis of defiance. Men unafraid to name the unnameable.

These parallels matter because they show how the crisis of the West is understood not in isolation, but as part of a broader pattern. The fall of the dollar, the rise of BRICS, the lies of Russiagate, the silence around Epstein, the endless wars in Iraq and Ukraine. These are not separate scandals. They are symptoms of a civilisation that has forgotten its soul.

Mappin and Carlson independently, and each in their own way, are trying to remind it.

The Platform to Match the Moment

And this dynamic is about to grow stronger. Mappin has already begun work on a bold new venture. A UK-based media platform styled in the same mould as Tucker's own network. The aim is simple but seismic, to create a space in Britain where truth can be spoken without apology, where sacred cows can be slaughtered on air, and where the suffocating grip of legacy media can be broken.

The potential reach is enormous. Mappin brings to the table not just vision, but networks: deep contacts in Westminster and the British establishment, longstanding friendships in Hollywood, and a trusted circle in Washington that stretches to the White House. He moves easily between Nigel Farage, Charlie and Erika Kirk's Turning Point and Candace Owens to senior Tory MPs, between media mavericks and political heavyweights on all sides of the political spectrum.

It is this web of relationships, forged over decades, which gives the project teeth and the power to impinge.

For Britain, the timing could not be better. Audiences are restless. Trust in mainstream outlets has waned. Alternative platforms like GB News have already shown that there is a vast appetite for fresh voices and fearless coverage. A Carlson-style podcast, unapologetically provocative, powered by Mappin's global connections and grounded in Britain's proud tradition of dissent, will add yet another vital layer to that ecosystem.

Mappin himself sees it as a civic duty. He has spent years warning that without platforms for free speech, Britain's heritage of liberty will wither. This venture is his answer. A modern Round Table where the conversations the establishment fears most can be held in full public view.

If successful, and all signs suggest it will be, the project will not only enrich Britain's media landscape but also strengthen the broader transatlantic movement that is challenging globalist orthodoxy. Just as Tucker Carlson has become a lightning rod in America, so too could this British counterpart galvanise an audience tired of lies, hungry for courage, and ready to reclaim the right to speak.

Friendship as Power, Power as Responsibility

In conversation, Mappin often returns to first principles. He told me that most people misunderstand power, mistaking it for the ability to coerce or to exert force, when the truer measure is friendship. How many people you help, and how many would help you in return. He said the fundamental of power is friendship, and the fundamental of friendship is help; to him, that is one of the most important things in life, not a slogan but a discipline practised daily.

Mappin has told me that his understanding of black propaganda, the weaponised art of smearing people and movements, taught him how reputations and even nations are broken by narrative long before they are broken by policy. He described how this kind of military-grade information warfare creates a 'leery sense' around a target, and how he set himself up to help, to counter those lies when he judged them to be aimed at America and at the West's reformers.

Closer to home, he has repeated to me the lesson Britain keeps forgetting: "When you take the king's shilling, you fight the king's war."

He uses the phrase to warn about local leaders who trade conscience for cash, drawing a contrast between towns that rejected central diktats and those that accepted them, only to find their economies hollowed and their social fabric torn. In his telling, sovereignty is not an abstraction; it is the unbuyable character of a place, and once sold, it is costly to recover.

A Fellowship, Not a Bloc

The historical record shows that the deepest ties between Britain and America have often been forged not only by treaties and formal diplomacy but also by human relationships. Before the First World War, Theodore (Teddy) Roosevelt and Lord Edward Grey, also a Wykhamist (as is Mappin), the then Foreign Secretary cultivated an intimacy during a walk down the banks of the River Itchen comparing British and US bird songs. They were both 'Twitchers' (Birdwatchers).

On June 9, 1910, the day before Roosevelt was due to sail home from England, the pair of avid birdwatchers travelled to the Itchen Valley where Grey had a cottage, for a day of birdwatching. They wished to compare British and American bird song and melody. They observed that only the golden crested wren or Goldcrest had a similar song on both sides of the Atlantic. Their walk shaped the Allied cause and gave birth to the idea of a special relationship between the USA and the UK.

In the 1980s, Thatcher and Reagan revived that partnership with a new ideological edge, declaring war on communism and championing markets, sovereignty, and shared strength. These were official leaders on the world stage, but their true power lay in their ability to inspire one another, to bridge cultures, and to galvanise their respective peoples with a common purpose.

Mappin's role may not carry the title of prime minister, president, or

Foreign Secretary, but in many ways it operates in the same lineage. He is not bound by diplomatic cables or political caution. He speaks as freely to American senators as he does to British backbenchers, and his conversations often cut through the suffocating fog of bureaucracy. In a time when leaders seem paralysed by polling and media optics, Mappin embodies the old Churchillian dictum that sometimes one must tell the truth to power even if the truth is uncomfortable. Although his style is more akin to Lord Grey's peace creating and peaceful intentions than that of the rather bellicose and often enmity creating Churchill.

If Thatcher and Reagan used their rapport to counter the Soviet bloc, Mappin and his transatlantic allies are using theirs to counter a different tyranny. The creeping authoritarianism of globalism, corporate censorship, and cultural erasure.

This is why Camelot Castle has become more than a Cornish landmark. It is a meeting ground where conversations carry the weight of history. The courage to imagine alternatives to decline, and in the will to say the unsayable when others fall silent. That tradition of Anglo-American solidarity lives on, not only through governments but through individuals willing to shoulder the burden of keeping the flame alive.

What makes Mappin unique is not just his courage but his connectivity. He is, by temperament and by circumstance, a connector of worlds that rarely meet. He moves easily between the gilded salons of the British aristocracy and the campaign rallies of American populists. He is equally at home in Hollywood as he is in Westminster. He has dined with actors, debated with politicians, and strategised with grassroots activists. In an era where politics is increasingly tribal and siloed, Mappin acts as a bridge.

This bridging role is not mere networking. It is about creating the conditions for conversations that official institutions have become too cowardly or compromised to hold. In Whitehall, too many discussions are muzzled by fear of headlines. In Washington, too many debates are staged for the cameras. In the Hollywood Hills, too many creative voices self-censor for fear of cancellation. At Camelot, those filters are stripped away. Guests know they can speak plainly, and in speaking plainly, they often find common ground that surprises even themselves. Mappin has seen time and again that when people of influence are allowed to drop the mask in private, the real work of problem-solving and alliance-building begins.

There is also a philosophical thread running through this. Mappin has long argued that society advances when free individuals, from different backgrounds and with different perspectives, are allowed to collide in honest dialogue. Truth emerges from friction, not conformity. That is why he is so dismissive of the cancel-culture orthodoxy, which seeks to reduce debate to slogans and diagnosis. In his world, disagreement is not a threat but a gift, because it sharpens the mind and strengthens the spirit. Camelot Castle, in that sense, is more of a cultural laboratory than a hotel: a place where new ideas can be tested, refined, and sometimes launched into the wider bloodstream of global discourse.

For Britain, this matters more than many realise. The country that once commanded an empire now risks shrinking into irrelevance if it does not rediscover its voice. As America wrestles with its internal demons and as BRICS carves out a new multipolar order, Britain's place in the world is neither guaranteed by nostalgia nor secured by treaties. It must be re-earned, daily, through boldness, innovation, and clarity. Westminster has too often failed in that task, consumed by short-term squabbles and paralysed by fear of upsetting Brussels, Washington, or anyone else.

Mappin's work demonstrates that influence does not always flow from cabinet offices. It flows from conviction. It flows from the willingness to stand at Tintagel and remind the world that Britain is not finished, that its heritage of liberty and candour still has something to offer a weary planet. In that sense, Camelot is both symbol and strategy. A symbol of a mythic past where knights defended honour, and strategy for a present where truth must be defended with the same courage.

The stakes could not be higher. If Britain retreats into silence, it will find itself reduced to a footnote in the multipolar world now emerging. But if it embraces its heritage, it can once again be a beacon. Not through empire, not through armies, but through moral courage and intellectual clarity. That is the path Mappin has chosen: to amplify Britain's voice on the world stage not by waiting for officialdom to act, but by acting himself.

In this, the transatlantic link is indispensable. Just as Lord Grey needed Roosevelt, and Thatcher needed Reagan, so too does Britain today need partners across the Atlantic who share its concern for liberty and sovereignty. Charlie Kirk was one such voice, a kindred spirit in the fight against lies and the drift toward tyranny. But he is not alone. A new generation of American and British voices, from state legislators to cultural creators, is rising.

Mappin is in their midst, building the bridges that may yet carry the West across this turbulent river. But also finding new voices. When we met last, he was cultivating new voices for freedom on both this side and the other side of the Atlantic.

To speak of BRICS is to speak of economics, yes, but also of philosophy. To speak of Tucker Carlson is to speak of media, yes, but also of courage.

The deeper truth is that these are chapters in the same story. The story of a civilisation that must decide whether to renew itself or to collapse under the weight of its own contradictions. And in that decision, Britain cannot be absent. Camelot Castle cannot be silent.

Mappin knows that he is only one man, one voice, one connector in a vast network of forces. Yet history shows that sometimes it is precisely such figures who tip the scales. A private citizen with the courage to speak may achieve what entire ministries cannot. A solitary castle on a Cornish cliff may host conversations that outlast the headlines of Westminster and the press briefings of Washington. That is the paradox, and the promise, of Mappin's role in this unfolding drama.

The world is realigning. The old certainties are dying. But as long as voices like Mappin's ring out across the Atlantic, the great tradition of liberty, candour, and courage will not die with them.

CHAPTER FOURTEEN

The New Round Table and the Future of Britain

Where Myth Meets Power

In the old stories, the hero does not always ascend the throne. Sometimes he stands beside it. Sometimes he lends his sword or his counsel to the king, ensuring that the realm does not collapse before its renewal. Beowulf serves in this role when he defends King Hrothgar's hall from the monster Grendel, fighting not for his own crown but for the preservation of another man's kingdom.

John Mappin inhabits this archetypal space. He is not a kingmaker, nor does he seek a throne. Rather, he is the companion hero, the friend of those who would be friends of Britain. He stands beside, not above; his role is to hold the line, to guard the flame, to ensure that those who might lead do so with the ground cleared of deception and with truth as their compass.

And in Britain, it is not a king we seek but a leader. If a new leader should emerge, perhaps a figure like Nigel Farage, perhaps another, Mappin's part is not to choose him, nor to enthrone him, but to ensure that the stage is set. For leadership in an age of crisis is never born in comfort; it is forged at the edge of chaos. When a people can no longer tell truth from lie, or courage from cowardice, the nation's very order teeters. At such a moment the companion hero becomes indispensable. He does not seize the crown, but he clears the fog so that those who would lead can see the path.

That is the paradox of the archetype. The hero who does not rule may be the very reason a kingdom can endure to be ruled. The watchman, the truth teller, the one who refuses to bow to deception, he makes possible the conditions for sovereignty. Without such figures, nations decay into confusion and tyranny. With them, the ground is prepared for renewal.

Britain's Future at the Table

The route to Camelot is never ordinary. To drive the winding roads of Cornwall, past Tintagel and the jagged cliffs that plunge into the Atlantic, is already to step into a different register of time. Here myth lingers in the air, carried on the salt wind. The hedgerows seem older than memory, the churches weathered into the earth, the sea a restless drumbeat on the rocks. And at the crest of the headland, Camelot Castle rises, part fortress, part theatre, part living symbol of Britain's heritage. To cross its threshold is to feel that one has entered a place not bound by the everyday calendar of politics, but by something older and more enduring.

Camelot Castle, it could be said, is timeless. It sits outside of space and time. Here thoughts are eternal. One can imagine Elgar walking down the main stairs from room 117 where he composed his second symphony, or Eva Gardner walking through the halls with Lawrence Oliver, or Noel Coward sitting at his favourite table in the Camelot Dining room. Or indeed one senses, Rudolf Steiner the great philosophical seer sitting having tea at the round table discussing Anthroposophy as he did here on Sunday, August 17, 1924, during his final visit to Britain. The trip to the legendary home of King Arthur was a day excursion from his busy schedule of lectures at the Anthroposophical Society's Summer School.

I had already spent the previous day in John Mappin's company. He had greeted me with the warmth of a host but also the directness of a man who knows his time is rarely wasted. Camelot is a stage for conversations that matter, a place where people come not only to rest, but to think, to talk, to plan. It is a theatre of ideas, where the players are not actors but statesmen, journalists, thinkers, and wanderers drawn to this strange cliff-top citadel.

It was during that meeting that Mappin's phone lit up with a name familiar to all of Britain. Nigel Farage. The exchange was brief, unremarkable on the surface, two men who have known each other for years, arranging their schedules. But when Mappin turned to me and said, almost off handedly, that Farage would be joining us for lunch the following day, the weight of it sank in.

This would not be just another lunch.

The Blue Room

The morning of Farage's arrival was bright and brisk, the sea flecked with sunlight. Guests moved in and out of the lobby, unaware of the layers of preparation being set in motion. To the casual eye, Camelot was simply running as it always did. But I had been in enough political spaces to know what to notice. Security men, discreet but unmistakable once your eye adjusted, were posted at key points throughout the hotel. I counted at least six, each with the alert stillness of men trained to watch without drawing attention.

Before lunch, I was invited into the Blue Room, a private room on the ground floor. Its name fits it perfectly, deep blue walls, lined with paintings, heavy curtains, and the quiet hum of history. It is not ostentatious, but intimate. A room made for conversations that matter, not for show.

It was here that I first encountered Nigel Farage that day. He was in conversation with John Mappin and one other figure. The atmosphere was cordial but serious, the way old friends speak when business is never far from the surface. Farage has that paradoxical quality of seeming utterly at ease yet never entirely off duty. He is both the most recognisable politician in Britain and, in private, a man who disarms with humour and warmth.

On the mantelpiece of the Blue Room sat the previously described brass sculpture titled *Friendship into Eternity*.

Mappin has often remarked that the rarest thing in life is not money or opportunity, but the full attention of another person. To him, these conversations were rarer than gold, and that was why Camelot existed. As a sanctuary for undistracted, truthful speech.

Questions in Confidence

I was given the rare opportunity to put two questions to Farage in the course of that morning's discussion. They were questions that matter deeply to me, and to anyone concerned with Britain's sovereignty and future.

The first was about the civil service, particularly the entrenched power of permanent secretaries. These unelected officials, I suggested, hold immense influence over the machinery of government, often frustrating reform and tethering ministers to a cautious orthodoxy that resists change. What would Farage do, should he become Prime Minister in 2029, to deal with this unelected estate?

My second question was about the United Nations' Sustainable Development Goals, the SDGs. To my mind, they represent a technocratic framework that binds Britain to global bureaucracies in ways that feel not only undemocratic but inimical to sovereignty. Would a Farage government continue down this path?

I will leave it to Nigel Farage himself to set out the full detail of his policies in due course. It is not my place to pre-empt him. But the clarity of those responses spoke volumes. Here was a man who understood both the frustrations and the hopes of those who feel Britain must be unshackled from bureaucratic capture.

The Lunch

When the time came, we moved from the Blue Room into the main dining hall on the ground floor. The space itself has a grandeur befitting Camelot: high windows that flood the room with light, a sweeping view of the sea, and an atmosphere that somehow manages to be both regal and welcoming.

Lunch with Farage was not a rally or a staged performance. It was, in one sense, simply a meal: good food, good wine, easy conversation. My family were present, my wife, Sundeep, and our twin daughters, Luna and Star. This lent the occasion a warmth and humanity that grounded the atmosphere. Yet even with that domestic touch, the gathering carried a strategic weight. Between the courses, the talk ranged widely, politics, culture, history, the state of Britain, the state of the world. Farage spoke with the candour of a man who has little left to prove, but still much left to do.

What struck me most was the blend of intimacy and consequence. Here was a man who may well be Britain's next Prime Minister, speaking not from a podium but across a table, sharing thoughts that ranged from the tactical to the philosophical. The presence of security underscored the stakes. The conversation, though genial, was never trivial.

Mappin has often observed that the great shifts do not begin with grand gestures but with small, daily victories. One misaligned brick can make a wall tilt; one daily habit can steady a soul. For him, sanity begins in the small things, and politics, if it is to mean anything, must be rooted in that steadiness.

Camelot as Nexus

It became clear to me that what I was witnessing was not an isolated event. Camelot Castle has become a nexus for precisely these kinds of meetings: a place where the formalities of Westminster are stripped away, and conversations of consequence can unfold in private, without the glare of cameras or the strictures of protocol.

John Mappin has built a space where political, cultural, and media figures can meet across boundaries of party and nation. From American commentators to British grandees, from foreign diplomats to grassroots activists, Camelot has become a crossroads.

He has even spoken of his own nation in mythic terms, saying that the British are an 11th hour nation, tending to rally at a quarter to twelve. Camelot itself is a watchtower against that midnight, a place where conversations may delay or avert the stroke of doom.

I witnessed only a fragment of it that day. Other conversations unfolded that I will not repeat here. But the pattern was unmistakable: Camelot is a node in a larger network, one that links Cornwall to Washington, Westminster, and beyond.

The Restoration of Sanity

What emerged most forcefully from that day's conversations was the theme of restoration, not simply political reform, but the restoration of sanity to Britain's public life. Both Farage and Mappin, each in his way, recognise that much of what passes for governance in this country has lost touch with reality. Policy is too often made for the comfort of international bureaucrats, the approval of global institutions, or the sensibilities of media elites, rather than for the lived interests of the British people.

Immigration is perhaps the clearest example. Britain has seen record levels of legal and illegal migration in recent years, stretching public services, transforming communities, and undermining confidence in government promises. The political class speaks in euphemisms about, 'managed flows,' and, 'humanitarian responsibilities.' But ordinary citizens know the reality. Border control has broken down, and with it, trust in the system.

Farage has long been the lone voice willing to say this aloud. At Camelot, his remarks left no doubt that he sees immigration not just as a policy challenge, but as a question of sovereignty and sanity. A government that cannot control its borders, he argued, cannot claim to govern in any meaningful sense. To restore order is to restore trust. And to restore trust is to restore the very possibility of democracy.

Mappin's perspective complements this. He sees immigration not only in terms of numbers and laws, but as part of a broader cultural and spiritual question: what does it mean to be a people? To have a heritage worth defending? He insists that compassion and hospitality are not incompatible with sovereignty, but they must be ordered by truth and by the consent of the governed. Otherwise, compassion becomes coercion, and hospitality becomes surrender.

The restoration of sanity goes beyond immigration. It touches education, where ideological capture has crowded out intellectual freedom. It touches media, where dissent is pathologised as, 'misinformation.'

And it touches foreign policy, where endless entanglements abroad are pursued while the home front crumbles.

Sanity, in this context, is not a vague aspiration. It is a return to first principles: that the people are sovereign, that truth is not negotiable, and that government exists to serve, not to rule.

Here Mappin's philosophy takes on a near prophetic tone. He has told me that true restoration begins in the human heart, with the courage to claim one's own happiness, to practise gratitude when the world trades in despair, to build strength through small victories, and to surround oneself with fellowship rather than isolation. These inner disciplines mirror the outer disciplines of nations. A Britain that remembers these things will awaken again.

And so the conversation in that Cornish dining room seemed to point beyond policy. It was about the possibility of Britain's renewal, the reawakening of a people long mocked for their traditions, long scorned for their stubbornness, yet still, at the eleventh hour, able to rally and rise. If sanity returns, it will be because men and women chose not to surrender their minds, their friendships, or their faith to those who profit from chaos.

The Transatlantic Dimension

What unfolded in Camelot that day was not only about Britain. It was also about the transatlantic conversation in which Britain is increasingly enmeshed. The presence of Farage at Camelot underscored how deeply linked the futures of Britain and America have become.

Farage is already a familiar figure in the United States. His friendship with President Donald Trump is well known, as is his resonance with American audiences who see in him a kindred spirit. Blunt, fearless, insurgent. At Camelot, his analysis of bureaucracy and sovereignty sounded as relevant to Washington as to Westminster.

Mappin, too, but with a different style, plays a transatlantic role. From his home in Tintagel, he has built connections that stretch from the White House to Hollywood, from Capitol Hill to the alternative media platforms that increasingly shape American opinion. These are not superficial ties. They are part of a growing network of figures on both sides of the Atlantic who see the crisis of the West as shared, and who are working, in their own ways, toward renewal.

Camelot, then, becomes not just a Cornish landmark, but a node in a transatlantic alliance of dissent. Conversations that begin in the Blue Room echo in Washington. Insights exchanged over lunch inform speeches on American stages. And the traffic flows both ways. Ideas and strategies cross the Atlantic as freely as data cables, knitting together a movement that is neither narrowly British nor narrowly American, but civilisational in scope.

A Fellowship of Knights

To witness Farage and Mappin together at Camelot was to see the convergence of forces that could shape Britain's future. But it was also to glimpse something much larger, the gathering of a new fellowship.

Camelot is alive. A place where heritage and politics meet, where the past informs the future, and where conversations of consequence unfold behind closed doors but with an eye to the destiny of nations. Farage may yet be Prime Minister. Mappin may never choose to hold office, or perhaps he will, but his role as convener, facilitator, and custodian of dialogue proves no less significant.

If Britain is to be restored to sanity, if the West is to rediscover its soul, it will be because men like Farage and Mappin insisted that conversations still matter, that sovereignty still matters, and that truth still matters.

Mappin has also stressed to me that human beings are born to belong. Power, in his understanding, is never built on fear or money but on connection. True power is friendship, and the essence of friendship is help. That is the philosophy that underpins Camelot as much as its stone walls, and perhaps it is the philosophy that will carry Albion, against all odds, into her awakening.

The Hero's Charge and Albion's Call

Every myth has its moment of testing, when the hero must step beyond private fellowship into public duty. The conversations at Camelot remind us that Britain, too, stands at such a threshold. To restore sanity is not only to strip away lies and expose corruption, but to recover the deeper strength that makes a people endure. That strength is not measured in armies or in treasuries. It is measured in the spirit of a nation that refuses to forget who it is.

The hero archetype is never only about individual courage. It is about the way that courage awakens others. Mappin, Farage, Trump, and their allies do not claim perfection; what they embody is refusal. The refusal to surrender to madness, to globalist decrees, to the slow suicide of a civilisation that doubts its own worth. In their defiance, they summon a wider fellowship, one that stretches from Cornwall's cliffs to Washington's halls, and from private rooms to public squares.

Yet sanity alone is not enough. For a people to rise, they must remember what they are rising for. Sanity clears the ground, but patriotism plants it. A nation must rediscover not just its common sense but its common story, its songs, its heritage, its honour. Without this, sanity becomes sterile; with it, sanity becomes strength.

That is why the restoration of Britain will not come only through policy or through protest. It will come through the rekindling of love for the land, loyalty to its people, and reverence for the story of Albion. Sanity prepares the mind; patriotism inflames the heart. Together, they summon a people who, at the eleventh hour, may yet rally, and rise.

CHAPTER FIFTEEN

Voices of Sanity

A Patriotism Reawakened

S anity is not a luxury. It is the fragile line between order and chaos, the thread by which whole civilisations are held. When individuals lose their grip on truth, nations unravel soon after. And when nations abandon sanity, they invite collapse. This is why every myth, from the Bible to Homer, insists on a remnant. A voice crying in the wilderness, a prophet mocked at the gates, a fool who dares to tell the king he is naked.

To speak sanity aloud is always costly. It exposes you to ridicule, to isolation, sometimes even to persecution. Yet without those voices, the culture descends into madness unchecked. In every age, then, the hero's role is not only to slay dragons but to insist that the world is not insane. It is to remind his people that lies cannot feed the soul, that silence cannot heal a wound, and that sanity, though mocked, is the most revolutionary act of all.

We will now look at some of those voices, different in tone and background, but united in their refusal to bow to a world drunk on deceit. And in their refusal lies the possibility of restoration.

When John Mappin walked into the Reform UK Conference at Birmingham's NEC in September 2025, he did not come as a partisan.

Nor was it unusual for him to be on the move. Although Camelot Castle in Cornwall is his home and symbol, Mappin has never confined himself to its granite walls. He spends much of the year travelling, speaking across the United States, meeting allies abroad, engaging with politicians, thinkers and campaigners across borders. Yet Birmingham was different. This was not a private meeting or an international journey. It was the heart of Britain, and it was a chance to see with his own eyes how a rising force was reshaping the political landscape. He went not as a loyalist but as an observer, determined to weigh its promise, to measure its flaws, and to understand what it might mean for the future of his country.

The atmosphere was charged. Union Jacks and the cross of St George hung from the walls. The songs were not staged performances but heartfelt affirmations. Flags waved, not as imperial relics, but as declarations of belonging. Britain, weary of being silenced, was reminding herself that she still had a voice.

The crowd was not the usual assembly of political operatives. It was ordinary Britain: builders and nurses, pensioners and farmers, teachers and young families. These were people who rarely entered the arena of rallies, but who had reached the point where silence was no longer possible. Britain is not a nation prone to sudden outrage. She prefers understatement and stoicism. But when ordinary people fill a hall with flags and voices, history is already on the move.

Nigel Farage was there, as he always is at moments of national defiance. "Whatever my faults, I have some principles," he declared, to thunderous applause. The crowd understood. Principles matter more than polished compromises. He warned too of what happens when people are stripped of identity and denied sovereignty: "If you take away people's identity and their ability through the ballot box to determine their future, do not be surprised if they turn to extremes or violence or anything else."

It was a prophecy as much as a warning. The flags that day were not waved by extremists. They were waved by patriots, reclaiming their right to exist.

Farage added another reminder. "We should not measure everything in terms of GDP figures or economics. There is something called quality of life." The people knew exactly what he meant. Quality of life is not numbers but dignity, freedom, and belonging. It was these things they felt Reform was offering back.

What was rising in that hall was not rage but reason. It was not extremism, despite the labels hurled by critics, but sanity. The sanity of people who know that love of country is not hate, that principle is not prejudice, and that truth cannot be indefinitely suppressed. The Reform rally was a patriotic awakening and, more than that, a glimpse of the restoration of sanity.

The Trial of Thought

One of the most powerful moments came when Lucy Connelly walked on stage. She had not plotted a political career. She had not set out to be a martyr. She had written a tweet, clumsy perhaps, but words only. For those words she was prosecuted. A thought crime, a phrase once confined to Orwell's novels, had come alive in British courts.

The journalist Allison Pearson wrote in The Telegraph that Lucy's ordeal was not simply about one woman, but about whether free speech in Britain had a future. If careless words could be treated as criminal, then all speech was in jeopardy. The crowd in Birmingham knew this instinctively. When Lucy stood at the podium, they rose with her. They had felt the same chill of censorship, the same self-censorship in conversations left unsaid, the same fear of speaking honestly in their own workplaces and homes. Lucy became a mirror in which they saw themselves.

Her courage was not only defiance. It was sanity. It reminded the nation that opinion is not violence, that speech is not crime. The madness of our time is that citizens can be prosecuted for words while real crimes go unpunished. By giving Lucy their stage, Reform declared that the English voice will not be gagged.

She embodied an archetype as old as myth. Joan of Arc had been a peasant girl. David had been a forgotten shepherd boy. Esther a young woman hidden in a Persian court. Heroes are rarely chosen. They are thrust into the spotlight by trial. Lucy was an Everywoman Hero: no armour, no career plan, only courage in the face of tyranny. That is why the hall rose to its feet. Her trial had become their trial. Her courage, their courage. Her victory, their victory.

The Truth Teller Hero

If Lucy was the Everywoman Hero, then Dr Aseem Malhotra was the Truth-Teller Hero. Once embraced by the medical establishment, he had spoken on national platforms, advised governments, and been welcomed on broadcast screens. That changed when conscience compelled him to question the safety of the Covid vaccines. In that moment he crossed the invisible line between insider and heretic.

It cost him dearly. He was mocked by peers, slandered in the press, abandoned by colleagues. Yet his sacrifice gave his words greater power. In Birmingham, he declared: "The Covid vaccines have created havoc in the human body." The words rang out like a tolling bell. Truth always shocks before it liberates.

As previously mentioned, before I became a full time writer and researcher, I served as a headmaster in an English primary school. When

I raised concerns about the Covid vaccine rollout to children, I did so as an educator bound to the welfare of pupils and to the duty of informed consent. It cost friendships and professional capital. It also clarified my sense that the line between public health and public relations had become dangerously blurred.

That position is why I listened to Aseem with more than intellectual interest. We have not agreed on every claim, yet his insistence that ethics, transparency and proportionality must govern policy echoed what I had tried to defend inside schools. In the years since leaving the education profession, I have been supported by Robert F Kennedy Jr., and Dr Jay Bhattacharya in the United States, just as Aseem has. That support made it possible to keep asking questions in public. The change I now sense in both Britain and America is not a single conclusion but a renewed permission to examine evidence without being told that the examination itself is a threat.

The Telegraph itself has begun to report cautiously on vaccine injuries in children. Even President Trump, once the champion of Operation Warp Speed, has called for a full investigation into what went wrong. When men of such different stations begin to converge on the same truth, it is no longer a fringe question. It is the beginning of correction.

This is what I mean by the restoration of sanity. It is not a victory for one camp. It is the return of procedures that keep a country honest. Let evidence be shown. Let counter evidence be heard. Let institutions admit error when they must and defend their work when they can. Without this discipline, education becomes indoctrination and medicine becomes dogma. With it, a free people can correct themselves without tearing themselves apart.

The Old Guard Watches

The establishment could not ignore what was happening in Birmingham. Jacob Rees Mogg appeared. Lord Ashcroft too. They came not to cheer but to observe. The Conservative Party, tired and compromised, could sense that power was shifting. Reform had grown from a protest vote into something genuine, a movement of energy, conviction, authenticity.

Even the shadow of America was present. The tone of unapologetic patriotism, the defiant spectacle, carried an echo of President Trump. Farage had long been Britain's nearest counterpart to Trump, and his words carried that insurgent energy. "In Britain," he once reminded, "we have an open door to half a billion people. We still retain the ability to decide who comes from the rest of the world." That principle, the right of a sovereign people to decide their own destiny, was the beating heart of the Birmingham hall.

The flags in Birmingham were cousins to the Stars and Stripes waved across the Atlantic. Two nations bound by history, bound again by defiance. And in that defiance is sanity. A common sense that borders are natural, sovereignty necessary, and pride healthy. It is sanity reclaimed against the orchestrated madness of those who would dissolve nations and identities alike.

The Round Table Question

Camelot Castle had long been Mappin's answer to fragmented politics and ideas. A place where communication is the weapon against grudges, where admiration can be sought even for those with whom one disagrees. "There is no problem on earth that cannot be solved by communication," he has often said. But communication requires humility, and humility is scarce in politics.

I remembered the first time I sat with Mappin and Aseem at the Carlton Club in 2023. Back then, they were still dismissed as outliers, men saying what few dared to say. Yet archetypes begin on the margins. The prophet is mocked before he is honoured. The truth-teller is ridiculed before he is recognised. The guardian is often ignored until the threshold is reached. In Birmingham, they were no longer outliers. They were central.

As the rally closed, Mappin thought of the sculpture at Camelot called *Friendship into Eternity*. Its meaning is simple. True wealth lies in friendship, true power in loyalty. Civilisation rests not on decrees but on bonds of trust. Birmingham had revealed that Britain still longs for friendship in public life, still hungers for unity, still admires courage.

Lucy was the Everywoman Hero, bearing trial for a nation. Aseem was the Truth Teller, wounded yet healing. And Mappin was the Guardian of the Threshold, warning that the passage ahead would not be easy but must be made.

The Round Table is not yet finished, but it is beginning to take shape. In the flags, in Lucy's courage, in Aseem's defiance, in Farage's words, one could hear the first chords of a deeper music. The restoration of sanity. Sanity in speech, sanity in science, sanity in sovereignty. Sanity in the friendships and loyalties that make a people whole.

The restoration of sanity is not abstract to me. I have felt its return at tables like Mappin's, where questions can be asked without careers ending for it. If Birmingham achieved anything, it was this, it widened the room in which a free people can think aloud. That alone is a repair.

Beyond Partisan Lines

To understand Mappin fully, one must also see why he unsettles critics.

He is not easy to classify. Like Tucker Carlson, Candace Owens, or the late Charlie Kirk, he does not stay inside the partisan lines.

Carlson's interview with Vladimir Putin in 2024 outraged elites but raised necessary questions about dialogue. Owens has defied orthodoxies on race and gender. Kirk, though pro-Israel, provoked fierce debate in April 2025 when he warned Republicans against suppressing pro-Palestinian student protests in the United States. He argued that if 'antisemitism' became an all-purpose label for censorship, it would be weaponised as 'racism' has been, used to silence dissent. In each case, they were defending not factions but principles.

Mappin too has said openly that he does not want war with Russia. He is willing to consider dialogue where others demand denunciation. For some, he thus becomes a target of insane minds and irrational editorial. For others, he is indispensable for without dialogue, there can be no peace. Without speech, no truth can ever find the light of day.

Toward the Watchtower

And here the personal and the political converge. Mappin is married to Irina, a woman born in Kazakhstan and raised within the Russian cultural orbit. If he is the bugle on the battlements, she is the lamp in the watchtower. His instinct is to provoke, hers to preserve. His work is often thunder, hers the steady flame.

The next chapter turns to her story. For if Mappin is the public face of Camelot, Irina is its quiet architect. Without her, the castle would be only walls and myth. With her, it breathes. It heals. It governs.

PART FIVE

THE RETURN OF SOVEREIGNTY

CHAPTER SIXTEEN

Irina - The Heart of Sanity

The Watchful Flame

E very heroic story, from the epics of Homer to the Arthurian romances, reminds us that the hero does not stand alone. He may step into chaos, sword in hand, but without a counterpart he risks being consumed by the very fire he confronts. In myth, this counterpart is often the feminine principle. Not weakness, but balance. Penelope in the *Odyssey* weaves stability while Odysseus battles the sea. Even Christ, in the Christian tradition, is mirrored by Mary, whose 'yes' makes possible the incarnation itself.

The feminine counterpart does not always take up arms, yet her work is no less heroic. She holds the centre, guards the hearth, sustains the pattern of order without which the hero's battle would be meaningless. If the masculine archetype is confrontation with the dragon, the feminine is the tending of the garden that must be defended. Both are necessary. Both are sacred.

So it is at Camelot. John Mappin may sound the call, but it is his wife, Irina Mappin, who ensures that the call becomes culture, that the spark becomes flame, and that the castle does not merely echo with resistance but breathe with sanity.

I would go further and suggest that Irina also fulfils the hero's archetype in her own right. The feminine, too, confronts chaos, often in forms that the masculine cannot. In myth and history, we find women who step into the unknown with the same courage and resolve as their male counterparts. Joan of Arc rides at the head of armies, claiming divine vision as her compass. Antigone defies the king's edict in order to honour a higher law, facing death rather than betrayal of conscience. In the Norse sagas, Brynhild is shield-maiden as well as seer, her strength and her vision both guiding the course of kings.

Such figures remind us that the hero is not defined by the weapon in his hand but by the willingness to shoulder unbearable responsibility. Where the masculine form of the hero is often conquest of the dragon, the feminine form is equally profound: endurance, the bearing of burdens, the quiet but unyielding insistence on truth when all around have capitulated to lies.

Seen in this light, Irina Mappin is not only the counterbalance to John's thunder but a heroic presence in her own right. She carries the archetype of the watchful heroine, the guardian who refuses to let chaos overwhelm order, the woman whose strength is not noise but constancy, not spectacle but sanity. And in an age of madness, that is no less a heroic confrontation with the dragon than any battle fought with a sword.

This book so far has dealt with big ideas: psychiatry and its abuses, politics at home and abroad, wars of culture and questions of sovereignty. But the Restoration of Sanity cannot be achieved only in parliaments, media studios, or international summits. It must begin within each of us, and it must take root in our homes and families. Without that, all the lofty ideas in the world are noise.

Nowhere is this truth better exemplified than at Camelot Castle, and in the life of the family who have made it their home. For here, in Tintagel, the philosophy of restoration is not a slogan or a theory but a way of living: a marriage, a household, and the raising of a child.

Some figures shape a universe with force, others with presence. Irina Mappin belongs to the second kind.

She is distinguished, refined, thoughtful, and assured. One is immediately struck by an ethereal quality that is both physically beautiful but is also a reflection of a deeply aesthetic soul. A woman whose influence is recognised in Britain, America, Kazakhstan and Russia. Within the press she is often described as co-visionary of Camelot Castle, a patron of the arts, a businesswoman, and someone whose salon engages in the fullest sense of the word. Those who come to Camelot expecting only John Mappin's headline-making voice often leave speaking just as much of Irina, and of the atmosphere she creates around her. She is a consummate host.

If John brings the energy that captures attention, Irina brings the brilliance that completes it. Together they have shaped Camelot not only as a fortress of stone but as a living home of art, conversation, and vision. Their roles are different, but never unequal. Each is essential, and it is in the harmony between them that Camelot's influence has taken root.

Bridges Not Walls

For Irina and John Mappin, stewardship extends beyond Tintagel's cliffs. They have always believed that Camelot is not only a British story but part of a wider calling: to build bridges where others build walls. This belief has taken on fresh urgency with the war in Ukraine.

The British mainstream media, for the most part, frames the war in simple binaries: aggressor and victim, good and evil, democracy and tyranny. But the Mappins are aware, as many serious thinkers are, that history is rarely so stark. Jeffrey Sachs has reminded audiences again and again that the path to this war was paved with provocations too often omitted. NATO's steady expansion eastward, despite promises to the contrary; the Maidan coup of 2014, when President Yanukovych was overthrown; and the long shadow of Western involvement in Ukraine's politics. These do not justify invasion, but they matter.

The Mappins are under no illusions about a failure in diplomacy that resulted in an escalated conflict. But they are also under no illusions about the military-industrial complex, which benefits from every escalation, whichever side wins. Ordinary people, in Ukraine, in Russia, across Europe, never benefit. They bury their dead, rebuild their homes, and wait for their sons to come back from battlefields they never chose.

This is why the restoration of sanity is most urgently needed in questions of war and peace. Sanity requires history, dialogue, and the courage to look at causes as well as consequences. It demands leaders willing to risk bridge-building, even when the crowd bays for drums of war.

President Donald Trump, whatever else one may think of him, understands this instinct. He resisted the drive for new wars, sought dialogue with North Korea, and has argued for negotiation in Ukraine. Tucker Carlson, too, provoked outrage for interviewing Vladimir Putin, but his rationale was simple: without dialogue, how can there ever be peace?

The Mappins share this instinct. John brings clarity with defiance; Irina complements it with continuity and access. Her contacts in Kazakhstan, Russia, Switzerland, Paris, London, and Washington are not public boasts but living lines of communication, preserved because she knows when to listen and when to speak. Where others allow doors to close, she keeps them ajar. Where others shout, she convenes. It is not a softer politics, but a deeper one: diplomacy that wears the clothes of civility.

The Round Table, Revised

Medievalists will insist, correctly, that the Round Table was a technology of parity, a clever furniture solution to the problem of precedence. Irina has reintroduced that technology to a century that thinks equality can be legislated by email. At Camelot, the table is literal, and who sits at it is not an algorithmic sorting by status, but an act of placement.

Imagine, if you will, for a moment, Hollywood guests have found themselves beside Cornish gardeners; a Duke of the realm has been seated between the bubbly local beauty salon owner and a glamorous psychic channeller. A poet next to a surf instructor; an ambassador has discovered himself across from a local farmer, Etonian peers and a Chelsea It Girl who ended up jousting in conversation with Alfie Best, billionaire King of the Gypsies. This is Camelot's quiet politics, reminding the world that no one really stands above or beneath another.

But this is not only hospitality; it is choreography. Irina's hand arranges proximity until candour becomes possible. She can sit a diplomat beside a Catholic Priest, a Hollywood name beside the owner of Tintagel's favourite junk shop, and by the end of dinner they have discovered common ground.

Observers often reach for metaphors about John Mappin, the bugle on the battlements, the trumpet of defiance. With Irina, the imagery shifts. A lamp in the watchtower, a hearth in the hall. If Camelot is both fortress and sanctuary, her role is to see that it is lived in, breathed in, and warmed from within. One without the other would collapse into caricature: a castle of noise, or a house of silence. Together, the pair keep Camelot from becoming either a museum or echo chamber.

A Northern Light

Irina's beginnings matter precisely because they defy the lazy English caricature, that Camelot is a parlour trick of inspired aristocracy. She was born and raised in Soviet and post-Soviet Kazakhstan, within a Russian and Kazakh cultural braid that taught reverence for beauty and endurance in equal measure.

Her family heritage was not only cultural but political. One of her ancestors had been an advisor to the court of Ivan the Terrible, and her grandfather, under Stalin, became one of the most highly decorated non-combat officers of his time, recognised for his achievements in managing Soviet agriculture during the Second World War. He was Stalin's chief Agronomist charged with ensuring the food supply. Yet the family's aristocratic roots meant that survival under the Soviet system often required discretion, preserving a sense of dignity and lineage while conforming to the demands of the regime but always acting in patriotic support of the nation.

The claim you hear repeated 'born of noble ancestry, raised among the arts' sounds like a fairy tale until you see how it formed her practical creed. That aesthetics are not ornaments; they are nutrition for a civilisation starving itself of meaning.

In England she pursued an education not in art history or décor, but in the hard frame of the polis, economics and politics. A BA degree from Royal Holloway which made her literate in power, budgets, policy and consequence. The combination is unusual and telling. Beauty without ballast is fluff; power without beauty is a machine that grinds its own operators. Irina studied the gears and then chose to oil them with art.

The Eye

Every serious patron starts with an eye. In Irina's case, it was her encounter with British painter Ted Stourton that set a course for the next quarter century. She found the work before she found the partnership. First the painting, then the painter, then the project. An encounter became an alliance, and the alliance became the creative engine at Camelot.

In every hall and room at Camelot is evidence of Ted Stourton. John Mappin's friend, his and Irina's business partner, an artist whose paintings reach into every corner of the house. Priceless originals by Ted fill this home: in the entrance, in the corridors, in the private rooms. His art is not decoration, but part of the lived atmosphere.

When Camelot was acquired in 1999, it was not just a building purchase; It was the manifestation of a vision and a purpose. Shortly after their vision manifested, it inspired Ted's creativity, Ted's art: his colour, his light, his philosophy, was essential to that vision. From the beginning, they set out to make Camelot Castle not just a place of hospitality, but a home and source point of creativity and creative inspiration

Ted is not just the, 'artist in residence,' he is woven into the family story. His brushes and paintings are part of the hearth. And in that, you see something deeper. That the restoration of sanity is not only political, theological, or intellectual. It is relational. It comes from those who know what family is, what friendship is, what beauty is.

This collaboration between artist and household is not unique in British history. At Charleston House in East Sussex, the Bloomsbury Group once fused politics and aesthetics, turning a farmhouse into a crucible of ideas. Across the centuries, our culture has advanced whenever artists and visionaries shared tables with politicians, thinkers, and rebels. Camelot stands in that tradition, but with its own modern edge. Art not as retreat from politics, but as its ally.

I have written in other books, such as *The Hero's Voice* and *Wild Thing,* that imagination and creativity are feared by totalitarians. A creative population is difficult to control, for it refuses to conform to a single script. By the same measure, a creative and imaginative household is a healthy one. It breeds independence of thought, resilience, and joy. That is what Ted Stourton brings to Camelot: an injection of colour, energy, and imagination that makes the home not only beautiful, but free.

Castle Household

Visitors often underestimate the quiet discipline behind Camelot's atmosphere. They imagine it floats, like incense, the product of chance. In reality, Irina put together a team that manages the castle household: timetables, menus, budgets, thresholds, conversations placed with care. That team understands that truth is not only declared from platforms; it is nourished at tables, reinforced by routines, made habitable by rooms.

This is why her stewardship matters. Her team tends to the invisible ligaments of culture: when a guest arrives, how long silence is permitted before someone speaks, whether the window looks toward sea or moor. To govern these details is not trivial. It is to govern mood, and through mood, thought.

Camelot Castle was acquired in 1999 and opened to the public not as a themed attraction but as a living, breathing home. One of those rare English projects that refuses the museum instinct. Most restorations embalm. Irina's instinct is different: to restore a place so it can exhale. She calls it "thoughtful elegance," which sounds like brochure-speak until you walk the corridors and realise what has been curated is not merely décor, but tempo. The place moves at a human pace; rooms invite you to stay long enough for silence to do a little sorting.

Is Camelot Castle a family home or a hotel? A myth-factory or a business? The answer Irina gives by example is older than either/or. The medieval style castle was simultaneously keep, market, chapel, court, gallery, refuge. Camelot under her hand resumes that polyphony.

Afternoon tea beside a Stourton canvas; a veteran warming his bones; a parliament of ambitious writers arguing themselves into clarity; a diplomat blinking at the Atlantic and feeling proud to be British, they are real. For the price of a room, a guest buys an atmosphere available nowhere else.

The Work Behind the Work

In parable-hungry times, people want Camelot to be all symbol and no logistics. Irina refuses them that indulgence. Her team runs production, accounts, staffing, conservation, guest experience, safety. The thousand dull magnets that keep the compass steady. A castle is stone and myth; it is also boilers and insurance renewals.

Her political education shows here. She does not confuse intention with outcome. When the Home Office tried to institutionalise Britain's soul by turning hotels into migrant containers, Camelot's refusal was public and loud. What the cameras did not catch is the private steadiness: a woman who understood the cost-benefit arithmetic, the duty to staff, the fracture lines that tear small places when distant managers convert villages into 'capacity.' You can say no without hatred when you know exactly what you are protecting.

Irina's 'no' is not the bark of ideology; it is the sentence of stewardship. Not here, not like this, not to these people, not at this scale, not at the price of the village's long memory. The press framed the story, as it always does, around John Mappin's voice but the house that made that 'no' possible was her work as much as his.

The Evidence of Atmosphere

'Atmosphere' is an overused word in hotel copy. At Camelot it does not mean mood lighting and perfumed corridors. It means that children run faster than their screens for once, that a couple on the brink of separation find themselves talking like friends again, that a painter who had not painted for a decade stares at the cliff at dusk and returns to the brush with fury.

Irina has a curatorial instinct for these soft proofs. Ask her for statistics and she will give you names. Ask for outcomes and she will hand you a poem left in a room. She trusts the old arithmetic, that culture is renewed one gathered table at a time, one guest who returns and brings two, one artist whose confidence comes back like a tide.

As the official Camelot Castle website puts it, the home was restored to share both the, 'extraordinary natural beauty of the environment,' and the, 'extraordinary strength created when people of goodwill share their ideas and vision.' It sounds guileless until you see how deeply it undercuts the sterility of a culture addicted to apps and bureaucracies.

Grace Under Fire

It would be sentimental to paint this as an unfought victory. There were years when the British press decided Camelot's myth had to be vandalised. Irina's response was not to hide nor to play the publicist. She kept doing the work. She built and guided her team.

It is a very English superpower, this grace under fire, and it is not learned at finishing school. It is learned on the pre-independent Kazakh steppe in Soviet schools and as a Lenin's Youth Pioneer whose motto was, 'Always Ready'; on the long road from one civilisation to another; in the grammar of exile and arrival. Some people survive culture war by shouting louder. Irina survives it by raising the signal-to-noise ratio of reality until the noise looks silly.

If you spend enough time at Camelot, you will see John Mappin pass through a room like a gust of weather, and Irina arrive like the season. Their marriage is not a subdivision of labour so much as a duet, trumpet and cello. He can provoke a nation; she can steady a people. And when the roles reverse, as they sometimes do, the parity holds, he will offer tea to a stranger; she will take a line against a ministry as cleanly as a barrister.

John himself has said, when recounting the story of awarding Donald Trump a knighthood, that the idea was born in conversation with his wife. "So I said to my wife, I know what we'll do. We're going to give Donald Trump a knighthood. She said, 'Can you do that?' I said, 'Well, of course we can... The very idea that there are kings and queens or nobles starts with imagination in the first instance. Who agreed to these ideas? It was creative origination followed by group agreement and no monarch nor any government on Earth has a monopoly on imagination."

"Titles and labels are simply that and at their roots lie agreement. We shall have our own noble order."

It was offered playfully, but it reveals a truth. Behind the daring gestures, there is always her assent. His provocations stand not as solo acts of bravado but as the outgrowth of a partnership.

Irina herself has described John's role as that of a connector of people. She supports him in that vocation absolutely. This is no passive loyalty. It is a conscious recognition that his bugle-call requires her architecture to matter, and that his public risks are made sustainable by her quiet consent.

John Mappin has said publicly that his wife, "Helped shape history," in moments when eyes were elsewhere; the remark was tossed to Instagram like a rose on a path, but those who know the rhythm of Camelot felt the truth of it. There are decisions that cannot be taken without the house consenting; there are censures a man cannot outstare without a woman's interior assent.

The Quiet Record

Irina's influence is best measured not in titles but in continuities she sustains and alliances she enables. Around her, things flourish that politics alone cannot create.

She has given oxygen to hundreds of artists, shaping a programme that restores courage to voices the culture war tried to silence. She has overseen a restoration that turned a landmark into a living forum, a place where conversations breathe as easily as the Atlantic wind. Through her hospitality, books have been written, exhibitions conceived, reconciliations achieved, and movements steadied. Even her refusals, measured, firm, exact, have preserved the sanity of a community against the careless impositions of distant bureaucracies.

This is political work, though rarely recognised as such. For Irina is not merely a patron of the arts; she is a broker of trust. She places people in proximity until candour becomes possible. She has drawn threads between London, Washington and other international capitals; between statesmen and dissidents; between villagers and visionaries. Where others build factions, she builds continuities.

The lazy labels 'entrepreneur,' 'publisher,' 'patron,' 'hotelier,' all miss the centre. Irina is matron in the Roman sense. A figure whose governance creates public good. The networks she sustains, the dialogues she keeps open, the trust she lends across divides. These are acts of statecraft, though they wear the clothes of hospitality.

Camelot endures not simply because it is bold, but because it is connected. And those connections exist because Irina Mappin has the instinct, discipline, and authority to weave them.

The Family

If myth must be brought to table, let us serve it properly. In Arthurian lore, the blade of right is given by a lady who remains in the mist. She appears, withdraws, and the king is measured not just by how he wields the sword, but by whether he remembers who handed it to him.

The Restoration of Sanity is not John's quest alone; it is a household vocation. The sword is kept bright in a woman's keeping.

I make assessments about people according to how they treat others. When my family and I have stayed at Camelot, we have seen how John and Irina engage with guests and staff. They are warm and friendly to everyone, even when no one else is apparently looking. Nowhere can you read the truth of a household more clearly than in the behaviour and attitudes of its children.

At the centre of Camelot's life is Caspian, their son, ten years old, home educated, articulate beyond his years, brimming with creativity. He is not a child raised to be hurried or processed by the world's machinery, but one given the gift of time: time to think, time to play, time to discover who he is.

To watch Caspian with his parents is to see the philosophy of Camelot made flesh. He roams the cliffs as if they were an extension of his own imagination, racing with other children, inventing games, letting the wind write stories on his face. He hunts stags with his father, tuna fishes in Cornish seas, and salmon fishes in Norwegian and Icelandic waters, learns the patience of waiting on a line and the thrill of taking responsibility for what one eats. He is a country boy in the best sense, and as my own four children are country children, I recognise the mark of that life instantly. The freedom, the rootedness, the refusal to let screens or systems dictate the pace of the day.

I know good education when I see it, and I know good parenting. I say this not only as a father but as an educator, a headmaster, and the author of many books about character education. In *Rewilding Childhood*, I argued that 'if we want children to be brave, resilient, creative and kind, we must first allow them to live bravely, resiliently, creatively and kindly.' At Camelot, I see this principle in practice. Caspian is growing up in an environment where imagination is not stifled but set free, where resilience is forged in wind and tide, and where kindness is the default mode of his parents' dealings with him and with others.

There is a wholesomeness to it, an old-school dignity that modern culture has almost forgotten. A boy taught not to consume endlessly but to make, to build, to test himself against the real. His education is not confinement but cultivation. Around the family table he speaks with clarity, listens with curiosity, and contributes with the frankness of a child who has never been told that truth must be disguised to be acceptable.

This is the hidden testimony of John and Irina's stewardship: not just that they hold a castle, not just that they host envoys and artists, but that they are raising a child in freedom. Caspian is proof that Camelot is no performance, no clever publicity stunt, but a lived way of life. He embodies the marriage of tradition and imagination, discipline and play that his parents have worked to restore.

And here lies the deeper truth. Education and parenting are the absolute essence of the Restoration of Sanity. We can have all the lofty ideas and noble manifestos we like, but they will not make a shred of difference unless they are applied to our children. The real test of any philosophy is whether it produces free, joyful, grounded sons and daughters. My children, too, are educated at home, and I know the difference it makes. The ability to grow unhurried, unbroken, and unafraid. Camelot is proof of that principle. A household where sanity is restored not by speeches, but by the laughter of a child running free on the cliffs.

The Long Game

What is Camelot if not a long game against entropy? Buildings fall, rituals fray, nations forget. The correction cannot be loud forever. It has to become a habit. That is Irina's genius. She converts thunder into loyalty. The roar of refusal into the quiet daily yes: to grace, craft, order, neighbourliness, beauty, and the discipline of welcome.

Someday, when biographers tidy the era into plot, they will try to measure Camelot by headlines or controversies. The wiser ones will realise that Camelot endured because it had a beautiful matron as well as a master, a lamp as well as a bugle, a housekeeper of sanity as well as a herald of defiance.

CHAPTER SEVENTEEN

Inside Camelot - Voices of the Fellowship

A Household Against Chaos

Every hero in myth, from Gilgamesh to Arthur, learns the same lesson. No quest is survived alone. The hero may carry the sword, but he depends upon companions to carry the burden with him, to see what he cannot see, to guard his back when the dragon strikes from the shadows. Achilles had Patroclus, Arthur had his knights, Christ had his disciples. Their greatness was not solitary but shared, proven in fellowship.

So it is with the Restoration of Sanity. The work cannot be borne by one man's defiance or one household's conviction. It requires a circle, a fellowship, a community that shares the burden of truth and loyalty. Without companions, even the strongest falter. With companions, even the weary can endure.

Camelot today is not simply a castle on the cliffs of Cornwall. It is a modern fellowship, a Round Table refashioned. And here, in the voices of those who dwell and serve within its walls, we glimpse the deeper truth: that sanity is restored not by solitary heroes, but by households of courage and circles of trust.

The previous chapter traced the hearth of Camelot: Irina, the home, the family, the centre of sanity. Yet Camelot is not sustained by marriage and parenthood alone. A house becomes a household only when others share its life, and a castle becomes a fellowship only when loyalty and service breathe through its corridors. The true test of leadership is not what the newspapers say or the cameras catch, but what those who serve alongside you believe in their bones.

Here lies the Round Table in its modern form. For the myth was never about Arthur alone, nor even about Arthur and Guinevere. It was about the fellowship: the knights, the squires, the counsellors, the servants who kept the hall. The Round Table meant equality not of titles but of worth. At Camelot Castle today you sense that same principle: presidents and pensioners, diplomats and gardeners, guests and staff, all part of a shared atmosphere, equal in dignity if different in role.

And so it is fitting, in this final part of the book, *The Return of Sovereignty*, that we listen not to celebrities or politicians, but to one of the household's own. For to understand Camelot from the inside, one must hear from those who live and labour there every day, who know its rhythms not from the newspapers but from the breakfast tables and the private conversations.

This is the testimony of Marek Wojciechowski.

Marek's Testimony

Marek has worked at Camelot Castle for around twenty-one years. He is not a casual employee or a passing visitor, but a vital part of the spirit of the place, one of the pillars that keep the roof steady. He is Polish, highly intelligent, with a master's degree in engineering. He could have pursued other careers, but he has chosen to anchor his life here in Tintagel, in service to a household that he considers his spiritual family.

He reminded me, as we spoke, of Anthony Hopkins in *The Remains of the Day*: the butler who sees everything. Yet the comparison only goes so far. For in Ishiguro's tale the lord of the manor was hollow, a villain cloaked in dignity. Marek's story is the inversion: the master he serves is the opposite of a tyrant. Where Hopkins' character laboured for futility, Marek serves for meaning.

I asked him what he thought of John Mappin. His answer was discreet but arresting in its simplicity: "I realise this may not be altogether real to some people, but I have been a witness to it for over two decades, Mr. Mappin is a man who on more than one occasion has changed the direction of the world, as a result of communications that have occurred from this very room. Unthinkable disasters have been averted and extraordinarily positive outcomes have happened."

Marek continued, "Hollywood makes us believe that salvation wears a tuxedo and leaps from exploding buildings. But in reality it looks different. In real life such affairs and matters shift quietly and generally happen as a result of calm intention."

He went on to describe Mappin as a man with, "An extraordinary intelligence." Not in the abstract sense of IQ tests, but in the practical sense of perception, foresight, intuition and strategy.

Mappin, he said, sees years ahead. He plants seeds where others see only dust. He looks at life as a chessboard, with moves calculated not in days but in decades.

It may take ten or fifteen years for one of his insights to blossom but blossom they do. Marek gave examples. Years ago, long before Nigel Farage's fortunes turned, Mappin foresaw him as a future Prime Minister. Others mocked; he simply filed it under inevitability.

When Donald Trump descended that famous escalator and declared,

"I'm going to win," most of the world scoffed. Mappin did not. "I believe him," he said, "though no one will believe me." And so, though he is not a gambling man, Mappin placed a massive bet at thirty-three -to-one odds. He won £100,000. But the money was incidental. The point was conviction. The point was foresight.

That wager opened doors. An invitation to Washington, from a conversation with Eric Trump, connections that spanned continents. Marek did not tell this as a boast, but as an example of how Mappin thinks: long game, high stakes, faith in people others dismiss. This, Marek insisted, is the secret. Mappin does not see the worst in people, but the best possible. He looks for potential when the crowd sees only parody. And he invests, with time, with trust, sometimes with money, in that potential until it bears fruit.

Marek spoke too of Mappin's extraordinary gift for connection. "Mr. Mappin is extremely good at creating global connections," he said. "He finds not only the powerful but the friends of the powerful, the overlooked intermediaries, the quiet links in the chain. He gets to know them, sustains them philosophically and with kind intention, and has created a network of goodwill that stretches from Tintagel to Washington, from Cornwall and to other capitals as needed."

Through these lines of contact came Charlie Kirk, the young American conservative who founded Turning Point USA. Marek spoke of how Mappin encouraged Charlie, passed on ideas, gave him counsel. He mentioned Candace Owens too, another voice in that chorus. Camelot became a place where ideas flowed back and forth across the Atlantic from the Far East and the Levant, fertilising movements and opening possibilities.

When Marek spoke to me, he spoke of Charlie in the present tense. He had attended the original introduction of Charlie Kirk and Candace

Owens to the UK in December 2018 and had been a witness to how that event had effected the accelerated expansion of Turning Point in the USA and all that transpired from it.

But as I write these words, Charlie Kirk has since been brutally assassinated. The testimony I heard as present tense has become past tense. Mappin, as I write, is on a plane to America to pay his respects to Charlie's family. This is not only a political story but a human one. The web of fellowship that stretches from Tintagel to Washington has been wounded. A young man struck down, a family grieving, a household in Cornwall feeling the blow from across the sea.

Marek has witnessed all of these events and many others from Chinese Trade Ambassadors to Arab Royalty and Jewish Leaders arriving at Camelot Castle working to achieve greater peace and harmony in the world and how they have impacted the family. He also accompanied the family to Jerusalem with Charlie and Erika Kirk in March of 2019 where he witnessed key actions at that gathering. Actions that assisted in the successful progress of the Abraham Accords. Indeed Marek was also with Mr Mappin in Oxford in May and witnessed their interchange on the last occasion that Charlie Kirk visited our island of Great Britain.

This is why I include him in my exploration of the themes within this book. Marek has been on the frontlines. Quietly acting in service to the family, and in his extremely effective way, his service to the whole team at Camelot has enabled many of the remarkable events that have occurred there to happen. If my impression of John Mappin was either exaggerated or false, I would soon strip away that veneer by speaking with people on the ground at Camelot.

The Cost of Caricature

When John and Irina refused the Home Office's demand to convert the hotel into a migrant processing centre, it was presented in some media as xenophobia. Yet the staff at Cemlot are British. Polish, Romanian, Indian and more. Mappin's own wife is Russian. The house is a blend of cultures, not a monoculture.

The refusal was not born of hatred for outsiders but of responsibility to the community, to Tintagel's villagers, to the rhythms of the household, to the staff who keep the place alive. To characterise such stewardship as 'bigotry' is not only false, it is dangerous. It cheapens language, flattens nuance, and makes dialogue impossible.

The same distortion can be seen elsewhere. In the Russia-Ukraine conflict, complex histories and provocations are simplified into comic-book categories of good and evil. To question this narrative is to risk denunciation as an apologist. Yet sanity demands that we examine causes as well as consequences. Without it, wars are prolonged and innocents pay the price.

For whatever outsiders say, what sustains Camelot is not dogma but loyalty, creativity, and fellowship.

Caricature is the enemy of sanity. Nuance is its ally. Marek's testimony reminds us of this. He does not speak of Camelot in slogans. He speaks of respect, loyalty, foresight, and family. And in that, we glimpse a truth the headlines never print.

The most moving part of Marek's testimony was not about politics at all, but about marriage. He recalled the wedding of John and Irina on September 11, 2001, the day of the Twin Towers attacks. For him, the timing was not coincidence but symbol. The evil of destruction countered by the good of union.

"The marriage of Mr. and Mrs. Mappin," Marek said, "is a powerful connection." It is, in his eyes, a balance of forces: good against evil, creation against annihilation. He described their marriage not in sentimental clichés but in cosmological terms, as the joining of two beings whose bond held the line against chaos.

And it was also a union of cultures. John, English, Irina, Russian. East and West meeting not in clash but in harmony. Their household is therefore not parochial but international, rooted in Cornish cliffs yet global in spirit.

Respect and Culture

As Marek spoke, I realised again a truth I have learned as a headmaster and leader of schools. The culture of an institution is shaped at the top. If those at the top are tyrants, those below are miserable. If those at the top are fair and joyful, those below reflect it. Every member of staff I have met at Camelot, from housekeepers to waiters, speaks with warmth of the Mappins. They enjoy their work. They feel respected. They feel like equals. That is not common in the hospitality industry. It is a sign of leadership.

Marek embodies that. He is loyal not because he must be, but because he chooses to be. He refers to Mappin and Irina always as, "Mr. and Mrs. Mappin," with respect, yet he calls them his, "spiritual family." That balance, formality and intimacy, respect and warmth, is the essence of Camelot's culture.

And it is not ideological. Marek was clear: "This is not a right-wing community. It is a common sense one." That distinction matters. Right-wing conjures shrillness and slogans. Common sense here means rootedness, continuity, home, family, tradition. It is conservatism as stewardship, not as ideology.

Defiance Without Bloodlust

It has been a powerful thing to witness the Mappin household, and to test out Marek's convictions, within the context of the death of Charlie Kirk. It is easy to see the good in people during pleasant times. However, periods of turbulence, grief and hardship can often reveal another side.

The day before John Mappin boarded the plane to America, he had spoken at length with and been in touch with Candace Owens and others in the Turning Point family and team. Their conversations, he told me, were not ones of despair but of determination. Candace assured him that the fight is not over, that if anything, Charlie's death will be a catalyst for renewed conviction. The spirit of that fight is not the spirit of revenge. It is not bloodlust, nor the logic of violence that so often consumes those who claim righteousness. The other side, the side addicted to hatred and caricature, seeks to turn politics into a war of annihilation. Camelot's answer is different. It is a renewed vigour and unassailable thirst for the truth. The determination that Charlie would not have lived and loved in vain and to demonstrate an inviolable commitment to uphold his legacy of free speech, inspection of the truths of life, and the right of a peacemaker to actually make peace.

For the restoration of sanity, the weapons must not be guns or swords, but words and action. The true defiance is to keep speaking when others try to silence you, to keep building when others seek only to tear down. It is to refuse despair, even when grief would justify it, and to continue the work of peace with a fierceness that outlasts violence.

Erika Kirk, Charlie's widow, has made that insistence clear and mirrored these concepts. In her statement after his death, she said: "They killed Charlie because he preached a message of patriotism, faith and of God's merciful love." She vowed: "We will never surrender. The campus tour will continue." She promised that her husband's mission would not end, that the fire lit in his life had only been fanned in his death.

These are not empty words. They are the voice of grief and personal anguish but they are also surgically chosen with precision, to sublimate an unfathomable loss into determination and purpose. Of loss converted into legacy. They stand against caricature, against the lazy reduction of a man into slogan, and insist: belief, faith, history, culture, and courage cannot be cancelled with a bullet.

When I spoke with Mappin about this book, he told me that Charlie Kirk's assassination should be understood in the same breath as the killings of Robert F. Kennedy and Martin Luther King Jr., and the visceral loss that Britain felt when Princess Diana died. It has, in his words, "rocked the American consciousness." It has shaken him and Irina personally too, as the loss of a friend and a fellow fighter. "I consider myself to be thick skinned in emotional matters as they relate to the world. But this most certainly penetrated the primary layer," he said.

The gravity of the event cannot be overstated. Charlie has been remembered in speeches in almost every major Western government, echoed across media platforms of every stripe. His death has struck a chord far deeper than politics. It has pierced something in the cultural soul. When speech becomes a crime punishable by death, when disagreement becomes a death sentence, sanity itself is on trial.

The murder of Charlie Kirk is not only the extinguishing of one life, but a mirror held up to our culture, showing us how far into madness we have strayed. It is also a mirror to be held up to ourselves and to our families. Watching this unfold within the Mappin family, and how they have responded, only confirms to me what I feel I already know.

Habits of Sanity

The happiest people are not those spared from hardship, but those who shape strong inner habits in the midst of it. Camelot has lived this truth. The household has faced challenge. Yet its staff remain cheerful, its atmosphere creative, its fellowship intact.

Sanity is not the absence of chaos; it is the presence of resilience. At Camelot, resilience is cultivated as a daily discipline. The routines of hospitality, the respect given to staff, the loyalty between leaders and servants, all these are small habits that together form a fortress of joy.

Gratitude is central. Gratitude softens wounds and prevents grief from hollowing people out. It turns bitterness into resolve. This is what Erika Kirk's defiance revealed. Gratitude for Charlie's life became fuel for his legacy. And this is what Marek reflects when he speaks of Mappin and Irina. His loyalty is a form of gratitude, sustained not by sentiment but by recognition of goodness.

Happiness, too, is not a destination, but a circle of companionship. A positive circle demands courage: the courage to step away from those who diminish you, and the courage to remain faithful to those who lift you higher. Camelot is such a circle. Its Round Table is not a symbol only, but a practice. Different cultures, faiths, and vocations gather there, creating a fellowship that nourishes sanity.

This is what makes Camelot a contrast to the world's caricatures. Where the world divides into tribes, Camelot unites around shared dignity. Where the world cancels, Camelot converses. Where the world reduces people to labels, Camelot receives them as human beings.

Simplicity and Presence

There is also something liberating in Camelot's simplicity. Life there is not cluttered by constant distraction. The rooms invite stillness, the cliffs demand silence, the conversations unfold at a human pace. In a frantic world, Camelot offers something countercultural: the chance to breathe, to think, to return to oneself. True sanity requires presence. Not endless scrolling or constant outrage, but the discipline of being here, now. Camelot embodies this presence, not as ideology but as atmosphere. It is the environment in which voices like Charlie Kirk's, and the Mappins' find strength to endure.

Speech without action is hollow. But speech with action, even after loss, is a kind of resurrection. A movement survives not by silence but by persistent insistence. That truth, kindness, courage, and fellowship are worth more than comfort, more than safety, more than silence.

That insistence is the thread that runs from Irina's hearth to Marek's loyalty, to Erika's resolve. The Restoration of Sanity demands that we choose the harder path. Defiance at the cost of reputation, truth at the cost of comfort, loyalty at the cost of risk. It is the path of real faith, real virtue, real fellowship.

In the myth, when one knight falls, the Round Table does not collapse. The fellowship endures. Camelot's staff, its family, its covenant of respect and kindness, these are the reforged Round Table.

Every voice counts. A Polish senior staff member, a Russian-born wife, Cornish villagers, American activists, believers of different faiths. They gather around the table not as consumers of ideology, but as bearers of dignity. The home is not only the hearth, but the council.

The Round Table at Camelot is not made of oak alone. It is made of people. It is made of conversations that defy caricature and friendships that outlast borders. In Arthurian legend, when one knight fell, the fellowship did not dissolve. The others tightened their circle, redoubled their quest, and rode on.

And this is the point. Camelot is not a curiosity on the Cornish cliffs, nor is Marek's testimony just a touching aside. It is evidence that sanity is not restored by decree, but by the stubborn courage of households and fellowships that refuse to bow to caricature or despair. *The Restoration of Sanity* is not a metaphor. It is the task of our age. The reclamation of responsibility, loyalty, and truth in a world addicted to lies.

And here is the challenge that this book lays upon you, the reader. Will you watch from the sidelines while civilisation corrodes, or will you take your place at the Round Table? For sanity will not be restored by spectators. It will be restored by men and women who decide, each day, to speak the truth, shoulder the burden, and hold the line against the dragon. That is the demand. That is the cost. And that is the call.

CHAPTER EIGHTEEN

Albion Rising at the Eleventh Hour

Albion's Dawn

History has always tested nations at the cliff edge of midnight. The darkest hour comes just before dawn, and for Albion, Britain in her mythic name, that hour has come more than once. She has been written off as finished, weary, spent, or broken, only to confound her critics at the last possible moment.

This strange timing is her character. Albion rises not at half past eleven, when calm permits careful planning, but at a quarter to twelve, when time appears exhausted and the candle sputters out. She rises when others believe she has no strength left, when her back is pressed to the wall.

Such a rhythm is not efficient, nor predictable, yet it is profoundly English, profoundly British, profoundly Albion. To stumble, to wander, even to flirt with ruin, only to rally at the brink, is her peculiar genius. John Mappin calls it, 'the eleventh hour instinct.' Others might name it providence. Whatever its cause, it has carried this island through wars, plagues, famines, scandals, and collapses.

Now, as the twenty-first century reels through confusion, with propaganda on every screen, psychiatry bent to control, caricature displacing truth, and assassination silencing courage, Albion stands again at that threshold. She is weary, yes. She has forgotten much, yes. But she is not finished. The dawn is not yet lost. Albion is rising.

The Long Road Here

This book has journeyed through dark valleys. We began with psychiatry, where power divorced from compassion becomes destructive, where healers instead control, medicate, and label. We traced politics and propaganda, where dissent is caricatured, communities are misrepresented, truth mocked as an inconvenience. We examined trauma, loss, censorship, war, and the silencing of voices too clear to be tolerated.

The picture was bleak because reality has been bleak. Yet always, through the cracks, signs of sanity have broken through: families raising children in freedom, artists refusing to flatter, communities resisting imposition, households like Camelot embodying loyalty and fellowship.

Still the crisis runs deeper:

Globalism seeks to strip Albion of sovereignty, folding her into a borderless managerial empire where bureaucrats dictate to peoples they do not understand.

Censorship smothers speech and thought, reducing citizens to consumers of approved narratives rather than participants in truth.

Cultural erasure dissolves the stories, traditions, and faiths that gave Albion her identity, replacing them with imported scripts of shame and conformity.

Economic servitude chains generations to debt and dependency, while oligarchs prosper and small communities collapse.

As we near the close, the task is not only to expose madness but to proclaim hope. The Restoration of Sanity is not fantasy. It is already underway. Albion, though at the eleventh hour, is at the centre of it.

Propaganda and the Hidden Third Party

Mappin has often remarked that propaganda thrives on false binaries; us versus them, right versus left, native versus foreigner. Yet behind the binary stands a third party, hidden, who profits from the division itself.

Globalist elites do not thrive by solving problems but by multiplying them, then presenting themselves as indispensable arbiters. They foster identity wars, class conflict, and culture wars, not to resolve them but to conceal who truly wields power. Albion's crisis is not immigration alone, or censorship, or economic strain. It is the hidden third party: those who enrich themselves by keeping her divided and docile.

Sanity begins the moment that mask is torn away.

The Great Disguise: Globalism as False Home

Villains in myth rarely appear with horns. They arrive as flatterers, promising safety, bearing gifts. Globalism wears this mask. It speaks of unity and peace, yet dissolves borders, erases identity, and subjects nations to the rule of unelected strangers.

Albion is told that sovereignty is parochial, borders cruel, traditions embarrassing. She is promised a seat in the 'family of nations,' on condition she accepts endless immigration without consent, economic decrees from foreign committees, and cultural scripts rewritten by lobbyists.

But globalism is no family. It is a hall of mirrors where each people is encouraged to forget itself, to trade loyalty for compliance, to become interchangeable units of a managerial empire. Albion's true homecoming begins when she tears away that mask and remembers. A home is not an administrative district, it is a hearth, a lineage, a story worth defending.

Censorship: The Banquet of Silence

When Odysseus returned to Ithaca, his hall was filled with suitors devouring his stores. Albion too finds her public square colonised, not by warriors but by censors.

Censorship today is rarely blunt. It does not often burn books; it buries them under algorithms. It does not rely only on chains; it silences with shame, job loss, cancellation. Speech is no longer tested in the open but rationed like medicine, doled in safe doses by governments, corporations, and media cartels.

But Albion's genius has always been unruly voices, from Chaucer's bawdy pilgrims to Shakespeare's fools, from Civil War pamphleteers to comedians puncturing pomp. A censored Albion is no Albion at all. To come home is to reclaim her tongue, to speak words others forbid, to laugh at the tyrant in his polished shoes.

Cultural Erasure: The Amnesia of Nations

A man without memory cannot return home. He may walk his own city and fail to recognise it. Such is the danger of cultural erasure.

Today Albion's children are told their history is oppression, their literature irrelevant, their churches relics, their heroes villains. Statues are toppled, curricula rewritten, rituals abandoned. What remains is amnesia: a people estranged from their past, unsure if they deserve to exist.

Yet Albion's genius was never purity but persistence. She carried contradictions: empire and resistance, conquest and common law, monarchy and liberty. To erase her past is not to cleanse it but to hollow it. Homecoming means memory. It means teaching children that their ancestors were flawed yet free, imperfect yet courageous, guilty of much but ashamed of nothing.

A nation that despises its past cannot rise. A nation that remembers, even with tears, can.

Economic Servitude: The Chains of Debt

Odysseus found impostors squandering his inheritance. Albion finds her wealth siphoned by oligarchs and speculators. Her people are told they are 'rich' because GDP rises, yet they cannot afford homes or families without debt. They are told to be grateful for consumer choice while industries collapse and land is sold to outsiders.

This is not prosperity but servitude: the reduction of citizens into indebted tenants of their own nation. Albion's renewal requires an economy rooted not in speculation but in stewardship, land farmed by those who love it, industries rebuilt by those who need them, wealth measured not in digits but in dignity.

The New Tyranny

The enemy this time does not arrive with armada or blitzkrieg. It comes cloaked and insidious. A digital panopticon that tracks and scores.

A regime of censorship where satire is policed as hate. An economy where homes are out of reach while corporations buy the land. A cultural revolution teaching children to despise their history. A global order whispering that borders are cruel, tradition backward, sovereignty obsolete.

These are not isolated threats but parts of one machine. A system designed to produce compliant populations, stripped of memory, chained to screens. Albion must resist not with nostalgia but with renewal. Not by clinging to what is lost but by reforging her identity in the fire of necessity.

The Prophetic Call of Camelot

Camelot Castle is a parable of this renewal. When John Mappin refused the government's offer to turn it into a hostel, he was not merely defending a property but declaring a principle. Albion is not for sale. That refusal echoed because it sounded ancient, the English habit of saying, 'This far, no further.' It was Ithaca reborn, the hall defended from impostors.

Camelot now stands as a beacon of prophetic defiance, proof that homecoming begins with one household's refusal. At this threshold, one man became a signpost. Mappin may never claim the word hero, for humility suits him more than medals, but in refusing the shilling he did what too many would not: he said no when it mattered.

His refusal was not only economic but moral. He saw what was at stake. The livelihood of a village, the safety of its daughters, the continuity of its culture, the soul of Albion. He knew, as his father taught him, that to take the king's shilling is to fight the king's war. And so he asked the ancient question: which war do you wish to fight?

In that question lies the kernel of heroism. Not in noise or wealth or recognition, but in conscience. Mappin acted for others, and in so doing reminded a slumbering nation what it means to stand upright when every inducement whispers to kneel.

The Hero Who Inspires Heroes

Heroes rarely welcome the name. They know their flaws and scars too well. Mappin would point to Tintagel's shopkeepers, his Polish staff, Cornish neighbours, even friends across the aisle. Yet that reluctance is the sign.

For heroism in this age is not about capes or crowns. It is fidelity to truth when lies dominate. It is protecting fellowship when division is profitable. It is turning down the bribe that promises ease but delivers servitude. By this measure, Mappin is heroic, and more importantly, he awakens heroism in others.

His stand at Camelot proves that no citizen is powerless. One conscience can ripple across a kingdom. One refusal can inspire thousands. One act of loyalty to past and future can keep the Round Table intact.

Fellowship as the Grail of Renewal

In every homecoming tale, the hero does not return alone. Companions travel with him, loyal friends endure the night. Albion's treasure has always been fellowship: pubs and choirs, cricket greens and chapels, jokes that leap class lines.

Globalism despises fellowship because it cannot be monetised. Censorship fears it because laughter spreads faster than laws. Cultural erasure undermines it by teaching children to distrust their elders. Economic servitude dissolves it by scattering families across overpriced cities.

Yet fellowship is the Grail. The treasure that renews the wasteland. Albion must drink from it again. Neighbours must help neighbours, strangers become friends, loyalty be restored. Without fellowship, there is no homecoming. With it, even ruins can be rebuilt.

The Eleventh Hour Nation

"Britain rallies at a quarter to twelve," Mappin says. "We wait, we endure, we absorb, but at the last moment, we rise." This is no apology for procrastination. It is our national character.

The British tolerate much. They endure slights, insults, and injustice. But when the cliff edge looms, when the fire reaches the doorstep, they rouse and resist. The pattern is ancient: Agincourt, Trafalgar, Dunkirk, the Blitz, the abolition of slavery, the stubborn defence of liberty against empire and tyranny alike. Albion's hour is always late, yet it always comes.

Now again the clock nears midnight. Despair is easy, for despair requires no courage. It is fashionable to sneer at patriotism, to mock tradition, to call collapse inevitable. But despair is cowardice in costume. The true antidote is fellowship. When citizens break bread, when neighbours laugh, when strangers become friends, despair is defeated.

Our fellowship will never be perfect. Like Camelot's sculpture, it will be rough and flawed. But if it endures, it will be enough. For despair cannot withstand even imperfect unity.

Albion's Prophetic Edge

To say Albion will rise is not prediction but prophecy. Not prophecy as fortune telling, but as summons. To prophesy is to declare what must be: Albion, remember who you are.

You are not a province of Brussels or Davos. You are not merely an economy to be managed or a population to be surveyed. You are imagination, courage, humour, fellowship. You are a people who rise when it matters most. You are the eleventh hour nation, and your hour has come again.

If John Mappin is, in my mind, a hero, it is not because he is singular but because he is exemplary. His story is not to be worshipped but imitated. He did not take the shilling. He chose the harder loyalty over the easier bribe. So must we.

Albion does not need one saviour. She needs a million small Camelots: households, pubs, churches, schools where citizens remember who they are and refuse the bribes of globalism, censorship, erasure, and servitude. We must all discover the heroic within, however modest, however mocked.

For in this twilight age, heroism is not an ornament but a discipline, not a flourish but a cost of survival.

Albion at the Eleventh Hour

Albion's fate will be decided not by metaphors but by choices. She cannot afford to be a museum piece or a theme park of old glories. She must decide, now, whether she will be a sovereign people or a managed province of someone else's empire.

The eleventh hour is here. If we remain divided, addicted to propaganda, ashamed of our own past, Albion will fall with a whimper. But if we recover gratitude, sovereignty, imagination, and courage to speak truth at cost, then Albion will rise stronger than before.

The Restoration of Sanity is not optional. It is survival itself. Let this be the hour when Albion stands, when her people recover fellowship, when her Round Table is re-formed not in palaces but in homes, schools, chapels, and streets.

If Camelot shows us anything, it is that sanity is possible. If Albion proves anything, it is that she rises late but sure. And so the call now is simple, weighty, political, prophetic: Albion must rise.

CHAPTER NINETEEN

The Restoration Through Friendship

T his book has not been written in the stillness of hindsight. It has been written in real time, as events have unfolded, sometimes at a pace so relentless that the ink was hardly dry before history turned another page.

When Charlie Kirk was assassinated, I received a message from John Mappin within hours. It was not commentary written after the fact. It was a raw recognition of what had just happened, the shock, the grief, the immediate clarity that this was no random act but a moment charged with consequence. That message, like so much of Mappin's life, was not reactive but prophetic. It captured, in real time, the gravity of an event the world is still struggling to process.

Now, as this book draws toward its close, another moment has arrived. On the seventh of October 2025, Candace Owens read aloud on her show a letter written by John and Irina Mappin. It was more than words on a page. It was a defence of friendship, a demand for justice, and a reminder that in an age of silence, sovereignty sometimes takes the form of speech itself.

The events and circumstances surrounding the assassination of Charlie Kirk are still unfolding. An examination of them here would not be appropriate at this time. Perhaps the next book will investigate this. We shall see. No, this is about Mappin privately reaching out to a friend in their hour of need and then publicly standing by her side during the darkest times. If ever there was a demonstration of sovereignty this is it. And if ever there was a truer example of the restoration of sanity through friendship this is it again.

Here is that letter in full, the very voice of Camelot sounding again in the present hour:

Candace Owens, Charlie Kirk and the Pursuit of Truth

When friendship becomes the highest form of patriotism.

Charlie Kirk built Turning Point USA on transparency, free speech, and a relentless pursuit of truth.

We are witness to that.

If Candace Owens had been assassinated, Charlie would have torn apart every lie and devoted every working day and night to uncovering the full truth.

He would not have trusted the authorities to deliver justice. He would have demanded it from the rooftops.

If Charlie had remained here, not the other way around, Charlie would have left no stone unturned until the full truth, the whole truth, and nothing but the truth was known.

Charlie would not have trusted the authorities to get to the truth and to ensure justice.

Charlie would not have waited for the funeral or memorial to happen. He would have gotten to work immediately.

He would have worked night and day to uncover exactly what had happened to his great friend.

Consider this. Charlie did not sleep for several days and

several nights just to ensure that JD Vance became the vice-presidential nominee.

And although that job was supremely important for the country and its future, it was still ultimately simply helping to secure a job promotion.

Candace is working to get to the truth of who killed Charlie Kirk and why they did it.

Charlie's execution is an assassination with potentially far-reaching political consequences for America and the world.

What we have seen so far beggars belief.

A crime scene apparently completely destroyed in days and plenty of evidence that simply does not seem to add up.

This investigation and the truthful answer as to who was really responsible for deciding that Charlie would be executed in front of the world will affect America's future, its collective soul and conscience forever.

The truth, when known, and we believe it will be known, will have far-reaching international consequences.

The very idea that someone could be convicted and could receive the death penalty when there remains even the slightest shadow of doubt or a shred of uncertainty that they may not be guilty of that crime, and that Christian souls would tolerate that possibility, is anathema to all the teachings of Christ.

If there were circumstances where a suspect or someone standing trial for murder did not have a clean opportunity to receive the very best and fairest legal representation to present their case and defence to the world, it would have been abhorrent to Charlie Kirk.

It would go against every constitutional principle he lived, fought, and died for.

Erika is in mourning. May God bless her and her family.

Please give her and her family time to grieve.

Any civilised culture, Christian or otherwise, allows a grieving widow forty days of mourning to make peace with the Lord and to respect the departed.

Those people who truly love her would gladly grant her all the space she needs. We certainly do.

But we are growing rather sick and ashamed of seeing people criticise Candace for doing her level best to get to the bottom of, and to the truth of, what happened to Charlie that day.

You do not have to agree with Candace on every subject that she addresses on her shows to acknowledge that much of what she is presenting on the subject of Charlie's death is extremely concerning to America and to the world, completely valid, and very relevant to the investigation.

She has an army of truth seekers worldwide who are helping her in her search and research.

This is a truly new and modern phenomenon that has never happened before.

This is not 1963, and boomers need to get used to it.

No one would question how bright Candace is, or that she may indeed be able to help her country get to the truth.

She is highly motivated to do so.

In our view, the official investigation should be immediately ordered by the appropriate legal authority to proactively share everything they know with Candace and her selected team.

That is, if truth and real understanding of who decided to assassinate Charlie and why is their sincere objective.

That would go some way towards restoring public trust in the system.

It is our view that her actions are not just the actions that any real friend would take for their friend.

They are the actions of the highest order of patriotism.

Candace's actions are service to the whole country and to the world.

Beyond that, they are truly providential, divinely inspired and metaphysical.

There is a relationship between truth and all living things.

There is a relationship between truth and God.

Right now, Turning Point USA is at a vital moment.

If we continue to witness the mistreatment and suppression of a young woman and a mother of four young children, who is doing everything she can to help get to the truth about who decided that her friend and fellow Freedom Fighter Charlie had to die, they will lose the country and the world.

And America will have lost one of its greatest living patriots only to see those factors against which he fought, and died for, win.

Candace's extremely valid point, that hers has so far been one of the only public voices from Charlie's closest friends questioning the absurdity of some of the communications regarding what happened and demanding clarity, is well made, and frankly that point alone is shocking the world.

We have been receiving calls from senior Republicans and from Turning Point donors who agree with her, all last week and, they started up again this week.

They agree with Candace but, seeing the attacks she is experiencing, they are terrified to voice their views publicly or to agree with her.

Is that really where we are in 2025.

We noticed that in one of her episodes last week Candace felt that she needed to state that she is not suicidal, whatever the word suicidal has come to mean.

Few people following the matter believe the official version.

A low minority believe that the current suspect is guilty.

That statistic alone is an awful commentary on the state of the official investigation.

The world wants the truth.

The world, Charlie, and those who truly loved him and knew his purposes, certainly deserve justice.

But justice needs not just to be done. It needs to be seen to be done, justly.

It must be truthful, fair, and clean.

"Trust me bro, I have seen the evidence. I was there, so you do not have to see it," is just not going to cut it.

If there are videos, show them.

If there is evidence, show it.

This is not 1963 and the world is not going to accept anything less.

This is not about who is right or wrong or whose theory is correct.

Candace's investigation is about actually getting to the truth whatever that truth is.

If the current theory for the shooter is truth. So be it. If that is a lie, then we need to know.

Every episode of Candace's show since Charlie died, from her heartfelt emotional tribute, to her exceptional journalism, has been incredible.

Anyone who cares for the truth and who wants to know who killed Charlie, for real, should watch every episode in sequence.

The fact is that what we are being told as his friends, or as people who had never heard of Charlie Kirk before his assassination, simply does not make sense to the vast majority.

It feels like gaslighting. It feels like we are being lied to. It is not hard to tell the truth to the public or to present the clear facts that illustrate the truth clearly.

Many extremely ethical people helped to build Turning Point and all associated groups, Turning Point Action and Turning Point Faith.

Many of these people are existing as well as potential future donors.

We know many of them.

Ethical people will not stand for lies or injustice, either privately or publicly.

The existing and future donors who were friends of Charlie's and those he loved deserve no less.

But please spare us the absurd and evil suppression of suggesting that Candace should not be doing exactly what she is doing.

She is doing no more and no less than what her friend Charlie would do for her.

Her actions are far more reasonable and experienceable than an assassin's bullet to the throat.

Consider for a moment, the evil of possibly allowing the conviction of a potentially innocent party with the death penalty.

We can only begin to imagine the wrath of God and how upset Charlie will be if an innocent man were to be executed for his assassination, and what ill fortune would befall a Christian country and individuals that would allow this.

In this sense, Christianity and a leading Christian democracy are now on trial.

There is a special place in eternity reserved for those who would allow such an injustice.

We still, supposedly, live in a world with the right to a fair trial and the constitutional and legal right of presumption of innocence.

If Turning Point and those Charlie left in charge fail to stay true to the principles and purposes on which Charlie founded it, and with which he and Candace originally breathed life into it during its formative years, then Turning Point will end up like MySpace.

It will become just one more ineffective, rather dull, has-been activity.

I believe that God has other plans for Charlie and for his legacy.

A cover-up of the truth is not, in my view, part of God's plan.

Nor is it the Christian thing to do, whatever denomination of Christianity you may subscribe to.

I believe that people of goodwill from all over the world will ensure that.

Keep going, Candace.

Charlie is walking with you every step of the way.

He loves you deeply and you are right about your friendship with him.

Never at any time, through all the challenges that the political arena and life brought, did he ever withdraw his friendship from you Candace.

You were, and are, an eternal cornerstone in his life and in his legacy.

What a great friend you are being to him.

We are witness to that.

All our love,

John and Irina

Candace Owens wept as she read the letter aloud. She admitted, "I needed this." In that moment the letter became more than words. It became a lifeline, a reminder that even in the darkest storms there are still voices willing to stand beside the truth.

Later, during her podcast on 28th October 2025, Candace commented on John and Irina's support yet again. This time she stated that their letter had "impacted the world," which indeed it continues to do so.

This is what marks Mappin apart. Again and again he has chosen to speak when silence would have been safer. Again and again he has stepped forward precisely when others have retreated. Sovereignty in Mappin's life is not an abstract ideal. It is lived out in loyalty, in courage, and in the refusal to betray conscience.

The mythic quest is never only about battles fought in the outer world. It is also about what is restored within. The friendships tested. The bonds reaffirmed. The sanity recovered through acts of faithfulness. In reaching out privately to Candace and then standing publicly beside her, Mappin demonstrated the true essence of sovereignty. The courage to be loyal. The courage to tell the truth. The courage to do so in the full glare of history's stage.

It was, in every sense, a homecoming. A reminder that sovereignty is not only about nations, crowns, and kingdoms, but about the integrity of a single man choosing to live by principle. This is how Camelot returns. Not in legends retold, but in friendships lived, in truth defended, and in sanity restored.

From here the quest turns toward its final destination, the return with the elixir, the gift brought back from the journey. But before we arrive there, it is worth pausing. For in the letter to Candace Owens, read aloud on the seventh of October 2025, we see the clearest distillation yet of what this story has been about from the beginning. The restoration of sovereignty, and with it, the restoration of sanity.

At the time of writing, Candace's video has been viewed almost two and a half million times on YouTube alone. The ripples and ramifications have rocked the world. Mappin's public stand of allegiance has now inspired other notable figures to step forward and show their support, along with hundreds of thousands of everyday members of the public. This is what taking a stand and having courage looks like.

And so the witness is complete, the stand has been made, and the world has felt its tremor. Now we turn to the final chapter of this mythic quest, to the return with the elixir.

CHAPTER TWENTY

The Return With the Elixir

The Hero's Stand and the People's Call

The return with the elixir is never for the hero alone. It is for the people. At Camelot, the reward is not abstract. It is the laughter of staff who kept their work when they might have been discarded, the village that walks its streets without fear of fracture, the children who still race the Cornish wind knowing their place is their own. Sanity, restored in one man's stand, becomes bread on the table and a roof unbroken by betrayal.

But the elixir is also mythic. Albion remembers itself through those who dare to say no when the world insists on yes. From More at the block, to Milton before Parliament, to Orwell with pen in hand, the line is unbroken. John Mappin stands in that lineage, not because he sought it, but because conscience demanded it. Camelot Castle is not just a hotel, it is a banner raised in defiance, a reminder that the English birthright is sovereignty of mind and place.

Yet the hero does not return so that we may admire him. He returns to awaken us. The elixir is not meant to be hoarded at Tintagel: it is meant to flow. Each reader must decide where their own Tintagel lies. Where is the ground you will refuse to surrender? What deception will you name? What small act of sanity will you guard, even if the world calls it madness?

If Camelot tells us anything, it is that Albion is not dead. Its cliffs still stand, its soul still burns, and its future is not yet written. But history waits on men and women willing to carry the elixir back into their own lives. That is how civilisations endure. That is how empires fall and nations are reborn.

The wasteland can still be healed. The question is no longer whether John Mappin has brought back the elixir. He has. The question is whether we will drink it.

Camelot Castle is not a metaphor. It is a working symbol with doors that open, a staff whose loyalty is counted in seasons, and a lobby where friendship is recorded not in relics but in photographs. A photograph of Mappin with Donald Trump is not a trophy, it is a receipt of myth made flesh, proof that corridors exist between a Cornish headland and the places where destinies are argued. The Round Table is not theatre at Camelot, it is a table you can actually sit at, where alliances form, where myth and policy meet.

When I met John Mappin in 2023, he had convened what others would not. Scientists and whistleblowers, dissident physicians and a Parliamentarian who risked asking forbidden questions, friends from the American and European right who came not to posture but to share a fire. That evening at the Carlton Club, designed for privacy yet destined for ripples, revealed what he does best. He is a connector, a catalyst, a man whose address book runs from Tintagel to Mar a Lago, not as an ornament but as an instrument. He gathers those who still tell the truth when it is controversial to do so.

The hero, in every myth, attracts allies. Odysseus had Athena, Arthur had his knights, Churchill had Roosevelt. Mappin too found companions on the road, men and women who, like him, had chosen to say no when obedience would have been easier. Tucker Carlson, with his laughter edged in steel, turning broadcast into a battlefield. Nigel Farage, who bore the jeers of Parliament to restore the nation's right to govern itself. Charlie Kirk and Candace Owens, young yet unyielding, insisting that gratitude and duty still trump cynicism and decline. And in Washington, a warrior whose golden showmanship concealed spiritual steel, President Donald J. Trump.

When the world sneered at a golden escalator, Mappin saw what was coming. The Excalibur Award he presented was not pomp, it was prophecy. It declared in the old idiom that leadership is sacred when it serves the people, that sovereignty is no sin, and that Britain could remember herself without apology. For that stand he risked his name and resources, because he had traced the consequence map and knew what follows when nations forget borders, sacrifice their children to ideology, or treat truths as negotiable.

In 2017, Mappin's connection with the President and First Lady was to keep alive the fellowship between two nations that best correct each other when they are confident. The point of a corridor is not to brag that it exists, it is to walk it when the hour demands.

And then came the drumbeat no one wanted to hear. A friend across the water felled at a microphone, vigils multiplying, the machine of misinformation roaring once again. Through storms of propaganda and ritual denunciation, Mappin kept his post. That, too, is the role of the sentinel: not to predict every blow, but to remain upright when the blows fall.

Mappin's fiercest claim is unfashionable because it is true. Ideas move history. Good ones lift, bad ones corrode. The test is simple, almost childlike. Does the philosophy dignify the person or shackle them? He has always answered by action, not abstraction. Whether defending his staff and village or defending the mind against the velvet gauntlet of modern psychiatry, his stewardship is consistent: protect the ground, protect the people, protect the truth.

What, then, is the elixir distilled? Not theory, not abstraction, but a code, simple enough to live by and strong enough to outlast empires. It can be spoken as seven vows, but they are older than words. They are the conditions under which any civilisation remains alive:

Truth before comfort: Speak what is, not what flatters. Lies unravel nations.

Gratitude as discipline: To give thanks each day is to remind the soul it is rich.

Friendship as treasure: Wealth is not hoarded coin but loyal fellowship, proven over seasons.

Sovereignty as duty: Guard the ground entrusted to you, household, parish, nation.

Courage without cruelty: To stand firm without becoming what you oppose.

Stewardship of place: Care for one patch of earth, however small, and it will anchor you.

Silence or prayer: In stillness, the mind remembers it is free.

These are my, your humble author's, vows. I may have been dispensed with by the state in my post as a headmaster for pointing out that your children should not be harmed by toxic vaccines, but I have never abandoned my post as a headmaster.

This is the code of my new school.

Welcome to Class.

If enough households bind themselves to these vows, the hypnosis breaks. Officials rediscover limits, papers relearn humility, schools begin to teach, courts remember their constitutions, and the old words recover their meanings. This is not mysticism, it is arithmetic. Sanity multiplies when lived.

I asked John Mappin for his conclusion of our dialogue and of hours of conversations and what observations he might have in conclusion of the past two weeks.

He was just home from Phoenix Arizona, Charlie Kirk's memorial.

Irina and John were most certainly changed, a spirit of universal revival was burning brighter than ever before within them and rather than looking back in sadness their steady spiritual gaze was firmly set on the future.

This was his reply.

"When observing good, freedom, beauty and kindness, validate it."

"Live every day with the excitement as if it is your first and engage in it with the sense of purpose as if it is your last, notice the beauty of all creation."

"When one views evil harm or unwanted conditions in any individual, group, society, or religion, anywhere in the world, know that not far away you will find a psychiatrist actively creating that evil or unwanted condition, or a person or being that has been driven crazy by psychiatric philosophy that has infiltrated the mind of that individual, group, or religion."

"They are acting out that philosophy to the detriment of others."

"One should know with clarity, only arrived at by personal inspection, that the correct target for you when you observe situations in life that seem to be a product of evil or harmful men, that psychiatric philosophy and its originators are indeed the root cause of that evil or unwanted conditions."

"Where you see any religion failing or in conflict with other faiths or religions, know that you are solely looking at the work of psychiatry or psychiatric philosophy that has infiltrated that religion. Churches and religious practice can be infiltrated just as easily as the mind of an individual and indeed at this time many have."

"Understand that the one luxury that the psychiatric psychopaths do not have is the luxury of self-inspection. But there are very few real psychopaths in number and once educated in these truths the world can recover its sanity and well-being very rapidly."

"What is it that such a being, the psychiatrist or the person affected by psychiatric philosophy is acting out?"

"Such a being looks at the beauty of creation and of life and declares either to themselves or to others that that beauty and life is not exactly as it is."

"This act, this lie, this blasphemy of life and of beauty, is where the aberration begins and with that simplicity, the fall from grace so often described in literature starts for that being. From that simple transgression all the ills of the world manifest in that being's universe."

"To the degree that others that are connected to that person, go into agreement with that lie and mechanism, and that person's fall from grace, well then, they are affected by it too."

"This is the exact mechanism that would be and has been described in religious scripture or later mythology as the devil, or the work of the devil, and this is indeed the function that precipitates evil."

"You can acknowledge it or not. You can agree with it or not."

"The choice is yours. See how you do with that concept and this observation."

"Does it help you or harm you? Does it work for you?"

"Acknowledging the beauty of nature and observing the beauty and benign, divine primary intent of all life and all living beings is an interesting way to start back on the road to sanity."

"It's a long road, it is an adventurous road, it can even be a tough road but it's full of charming and wonderful surprises. I do hope you have fun with it."

And with that, John excused himself and took off for an evening walk along the beautiful Cornish cliffs of Tintagel with Irina, his son Caspian and of course the family dog, Monty.

That evening was one those beautiful late September evenings that one gets in Tintagel at that time of year, but this one was spectacular, with the sun shining through the low hanging clouds above a still Atlantic ocean, shafts of light penetrating them creating Jacob's Ladders in the sky at angles cascading down in shades of yellow and gold from the heavens. One could almost see the angels ascending and descending as is so often depicted in paintings.

And just for that moment in that evening sun, I imagined Charlie, joining his friends in spirit form, on that cliff top evening sojourn. Laughing together, jousting over esoteric ideas and the next campaign, planning and dreaming those same dreams of adventure, futures, peace and freedom. The very peace and freedom that they had all laughed and dreamed about when they had walked the path of Christ together with Charlie and Erika in Jerusalem seven years before.

Monty ran across the cliff tops after a ball. Tail wagging and eager for the next throw.

John's deeply insightful words on the importance of seeing beauty in all creation will remain with me forever, for an eternity in fact.

Eternity and eternal life is not an idea that one often has the luxury to consider in today's rushing busy world. My family and I are truly grateful that we had the opportunity to do just that at Camelot Castle and to be able to share our observations with you in this book. I hope you will be able to carry with you in your heart, as a result, a little of the magic that truly is Camelot Castle.

EPILOGUE

'The Opposite of War Is Not Peace. It is the Creation of Friendship.'

I t has been, once again, a task to keep up with the fast-moving developments in the life of John and Irina Mappin.

While writing this book, events have unfolded at such a pace that each chapter has felt less like a record of the past and more like a dispatch from the present.

In the process of researching, several high-profile and highly positive features have appeared in the mainstream media. The Daily Mail, The Telegraph, and on GB News, filmed live from Washington, D.C., reflecting a united recognition of John's influence and message. As the ink was barely dry on one chapter, another extraordinary chapter began to write itself in real time. The death of Charlie Kirk, and all that has followed, has created a unique historical significance to these pages.

That is why this epilogue exists. It has happened again. History has moved even as the story was being told.

Let me say this very clearly. It is not insanity to want world peace, nor to desire friendly relations with those who are currently regarded as foes. I want my four children and my granddaughter to grow up in a peaceful and prosperous world. John and Irina Mappin wish the same for their son, Caspian. For that reason I will nail my colours to the mast and say plainly, I want friendly relations with Russia, with China, with the Middle East and with all countries. A global conflict would bring untold deaths and even the real possibility of human extinction.

The architects of such a catastrophe would not lie broken on battlefields; they would be safely hidden away in their underground bunkers. It would be the ordinary people on the ground, in the UK, the United States, England's towns, and across the rest of the world, who would bear the suffering.

You may remember the attacks Tucker Carlson received for his decision to interview Vladimir Putin. I profoundly disagree with the assessment that this was somehow wrong. We must hear all sides of an argument if we are ever to reach independent and accurate conclusions. We certainly cannot rely solely on the media to tell us what the facts are. The freedom to question, to converse, and to listen, even to those with whom we disagree, is the foundation of any lasting peace.

Suppressing dialogue does not preserve truth; it buries it.

Providence on the Road to Peace

There are moments in history so delicate that they seem to hinge on chance, a delay, a conversation, a single message sent at precisely the right time. And yet, in the pattern of providence, such accidents are never accidents at all.

It was on a windswept Cornish morning, the sea shrouded in mist, that John and Irina Mappin set out with their son for the airport. Bound for America, they were to attend the memorial day of their dear friend, Charlie Kirk, the Peacemaker Knight. They had left early, as they always do, with the precision of those who know that destiny seldom waits. But on that road between Camelot and the wider world, something curious happened.

A Cornish tractor and a bus that had got stuck, delayed them just long enough to miss their flight, the first time in decades that the Mappins had ever done so. And yet, in that pause, in the forced patience of waiting, another current began to move.

John has long been known for his extraordinary network of connections, stretching across the globe and across every political and cultural divide. He speaks with leaders, artists, innovators, and thinkers from every continent. People of influence and conscience who, whatever their nation or ideology, recognise the shared calling to build rather than destroy. Among them is Kirill Dmitriev, the Russian presidential envoy and financier, with whom John has often exchanged reflections openly on Twitter (X), dialogues that bridge not only geography but philosophy, faith, and statecraft itself.

As John, Irina, and Caspian sat in the car that morning, John began corresponding with Dmitriev, who is known for his closeness to the Russian Orthodox Church. Irina, ever the intuitive heart, had spoken only minutes earlier of Charlie Kirk's legacy, and of a thought that had come to her as clear as sunlight through storm cloud:

"Charlie's life was a bridge. Perhaps even now it can unite those who stand on opposite sides of war. What if the Russian Orthodox Church were to recognise him, with some type of saintly quality."

John took up that thought as one takes up a sword of light. By the time they had reached the airport, too late for their flight but right on time for history, a message had gone out to Moscow. Dmitriev replied swiftly. He would speak with the Church.

Within hours, word came back, not through politics, not through diplomacy, but through the quiet authority of faith. The Russian Orthodox Church, whose prayers stretch from the Urals to the Rocky Mountains and Alaska, would consider recognising Charlie Kirk's spiritual contribution to the renewal of Christianity and to the cause of peace.

It was an act that no one had planned, and yet everyone seemed to feel was waiting to happen.

Within days, Metropolitan Tikhon Shevkunov, publicly referred to Charlie as a martyr, praising his courage and conviction as one who, "Stood for truth when it was forbidden to speak." Russian Orthodox publications followed, including OrthoChristian, Izvestia, and Rossiyskaya Gazeta, describing Kirk's life as an example to modern believers and hinting at an ecclesiastical recognition that transcended politics.

No synod had yet met, no canon had yet been written, and yet something had already shifted in the unseen. A bridge was being built, not of treaties or trade, but of reverence and remembrance.

And it had begun, improbably, on a Cornish road, delayed behind a tractor.

John would later laugh, "God works through a Massey Ferguson."

In the days that followed, the Russian Orthodox Church reached out to Erika Kirk, Charlie's widow, offering prayers and solidarity. For a moment, brief yet eternal, the world's most ancient Christian tradition extended its hand toward the American West, and across that distance flowed something that neither governments nor armies could achieve.

The opposite of war is not peace. It is the creation of friendship.

Peace can be fragile, a pause between storms, a treaty written on sand.

But friendship, real friendship, forged in love and truth, is a covenant that even empires cannot break. It is rough-edged and unpredictable, but it binds where policy divides. It is friendship that turns enemies into neighbours and converts suspicion into strength.

That moment, Irina's idea, John's message, Kirill's reply, the Church's blessing, was more than sentiment. It was, perhaps, the balancing of the world. For as Tucker Carlson once warned, the West stands perilously close to nuclear confrontation, a sleepwalk toward extinction. And yet, in that slender space between pride and humility, between fear and faith, friendship can still stay the hand of war.

And thus it is that seeds of peace and sanity germinate and grow, indeed in the last few hours as I write and try to conclude this epilogue, new proposals by Mr Kirill Dimitriev are now circulating in Washington DC for a connecting tunnel to be built under the Bering Straits to join Russia and America, drawing on an idea initially floated by Nikita Khrushchev and John F Kennedy. This was immediately supported by someone who Charlie Kirk and Mappin championed in her run for Congress and began in politics with Turning Point. Congresswoman Anna Paulina Luna, who is now becoming a prominent peacemaker in her own right.

As you will have discovered within the pages of this book, it is not the first time such currents have moved through and around the Camelot orbits. There have been other moments, unseen, unsung, when a call from Tintagel has rippled through embassies and chancelleries, when a word of sanity has softened the edge of madness. This was another.

Charlie Kirk's life, and now his remembrance, became the axis upon which several worlds turned: America and Russia, faith and politics, East and West, the living and the departed.

Through it all ran the unbroken thread of sovereignty through sanity.

For Irina and John Mappin, this was never about recognition or glory. It was about restoring the human face to faith and diplomacy, reminding nations that friendship is not weakness but wisdom, and that no wall of ideology is taller than a single act of grace.

In the light of that truth, the Restoration of Sanity is not merely a British dream, nor an American crusade, nor even a Russian, Chinese or Middle Eastern awakening. It is a universal summons to recognise that the soul of the world still yearns to be healed, and that such healing begins not in parliaments or pulpits, but in the simple decision to befriend what one does not yet, at this moment, understand.

And so the story of Sovereignty closes as it began: with a conversation between friends.

Where does this now lead? I ask you, the reader, to consider what would be better for you and your family. An all-out world war, or friendship? To me, the answer could not be clearer. Often those we fight with are, after all, our former allies, brothers or close relatives. The same people who stood beside us in the fight against tyranny during the Second World War we now oppose in word and deed. Is this sanity? We will always have our differences, our arguments, even our scrapes, yet that is the nature of all true friendships. They are not perfect, but they endure.

Decide yourself what stance to take. Spot who it is that creates the enmity between past friends and allies.

Expose that evil.

Validate decency and goodness when you see it.

The future is not yet written, and it belongs to those brave enough to imagine peace. To those who dare to befriend rather than to fear.

For in the end, friendship is what underpins both sanity and sovereignty.

Let us not lose our humanity, not now, and certainly not when the world needs it most.

And so, from this clifftop above the roaring sea, the call goes out once more.

Camelot still stands, and friendship, not fear, will light the way.

What dreams, what new icons, what new heroes, and what great futures will come? Only you and those who create their future sovereignty can decide!

Printed in Dunstable, United Kingdom